Don't Vote For Me

By Kevin Hayes

DON'T VOTE FOR ME

By Kevin Hayes

Copyright © 2011 by Kevin Hayes

All rights reserved

**For Specialist Matthew R. Hayes,
United States Army,**

my grandchildren,

and

in memory of my little sister, Patricia Rose Hayes

"Things turn out best for the people who make the best of the way things turn out."

~John Wooden

TABLE OF CONTENTS

ACKNOWLEDGEMENTS	I
PREFACE	III
CHAPTER I THE ABSOLUTE BEGINNING	1
CHAPTER II THE SETTING	6
CHAPTER III A WICKED START	15
CHAPTER IV THE DOMESTIC CAMPAIGN BEGINS	22
CHAPTER V I CAN'T GET OUT!	33
CHAPTER VI MATTHEW 26:74	44

CHAPTER VII	49
HIP DEEP AND SINKING	
CHAPTER VIII	59
SIGNS OF THINGS TO COME	
CHAPTER IX	75
I AM A RACIST	
CHAPTER X	84
WALKING THE WALK AND TALKING THE TALK	
CHAPTER XI	93
I CONFRONT MY ACCUSER	
CHAPTER XII	105
HAIL MARYS AND SUPER BOWL	
APPENDIX	120
EPILOGUE	121

DON'T VOTE FOR ME

ACKNOWLEDGEMENTS

This is a first-person account of the events that follow, and unfortunately does not do justice in regard to the sacrifices others made on my behalf during the summer of 2006. I apologize both for this omission and the misappropriation of your time and talent that summer, but be assured this story would have been impossible without you.

I am especially indebted my wife Bernadette, and to my family; to Renae Larsen, my trusty campaign treasurer-the one and only authentic member of my election committee; to Jason Denovich, Christine Andrew, Jeffrey Van Camp, and Richard Llewellyn Williams. Without them, my handwritten memoir would have remained nothing more than barely legible scribbling of dry ink, indecipherable to many and ignored by all.

It is altogether fitting and proper to mention candidates Greg Carlson, Josh Nunez, Tim Black, Mike Trebesh, Paul Opsommer, Ron McComb and Rodney Hampton. We went through a lot together. I've done my best to be accurate and fair, and I've tried to balance any anecdotal jest from the campaign with abundant self-deprecation. Accordingly, I hope it may be said of me that I've remained nothing less than a friend to you all.

DON'T VOTE FOR ME

DON'T VOTE FOR ME

PREFACE

There I was, by the dawn's early light, standing in the middle of a half-acre field of chest high weeds and wildflowers. The election was only two weeks away and I had forgotten to bring a weed whip with me. How were people supposed to see my campaign sign in this jungle? I had to be at work in an hour and I didn't have time to drive home to get it, but I wasn't about to let this morning's mistake turn out to be another wasted trip. So I lay down on the ground, tucked in my arms, curled up my knees and began rolling over and over and over again looking like an idiot trying to put out an invisible prairie fire. Bemused pride came over me as dew-covered stalks and stems began to snap, bend and flatten under my body as I steamrolled my way toward northbound US-127. It was a short-lived sense of victory.

As I rose to my feet, admiring my name reflected by the rising sun over that field just south of Ithaca, Michigan, it dawned on me that I had totally lost all perspective. Almost instantaneously I admitted to myself that without a doubt this whole political process was insane, and somehow I had let myself become a willing participant in all of this nonsense. And then – right there– I began laughing at myself. Why was I doing this? To what end?

I thought of Walter Mondale not finding the beef in 1984.

DON'T VOTE FOR ME

Of Bob Dole waking up Bob Dole to inform Bob Dole that Bob Dole lost big-time in 1996. I thought of 1992, of George H.W. Bush, fire in the belly, and about so many other campaigns that never quite got off the ground. Why was I playing out the string in this nothing of a race? I knew I had no chance of winning the election. I was the sixth man in a five-man race and I had known since Memorial Day that I didn't stand a chance to win this election.

And so there I was. Just like them. Not yet quite off the ground either. Literally. But this was neither the time nor the place for rational thought, as I was motivated by my sister-in-law's haunting admonition: *"You can probably count on fifty-three votes from friends and relatives -the rest is up in the air."* So I continued in my folly rolling among the weeds all the more, with seeds and burrs and chaff sticking to my clothes and skin like glue, providing the physical evidence of my Plimpton-esque misadventure.

Yes, George Plimpton. He was a fairly significant Ivy League journalist who regaled America's baby-boom youth with his impossible quests for athletic fulfillment in the world of professional sports. Some of you may remember him –the tall, thin, but not especially coordinated author who became known as the Paper Lion. And now like George, I too have my own story to tell –a true story of a childhood fantasy gone bad. It concerns the August 2006 primary election for the 93rd State House District, an

DON'T VOTE FOR ME

area of Michigan just north of its Capitol city, Lansing. *Don't Vote For Me* is a different kind of campaign story because it is told from a candidate's perspective for once. Somewhat reluctantly I've decided to use the real names of eight citizens –six Republicans and two Democrats– who volunteered to give up anonymity to run for this particular seat. It just didn't make sense to do it any other way. As for everyone else- don't worry. I have your back. I will do my best to protect your innocence, and if not your innocence, then your privacy, and if not your privacy, your plausible denial.

So why take the time to learn about my quixotic adventure? There is an old saying that you should not judge a man until you walk a mile in his shoes. So that is what I did. Come on and take a hike with me. I'm going to tell you what I learned.

DON'T VOTE FOR ME

CHAPTER I

THE ABSOLUTE BEGINNING

At the outset let me be perfectly clear: I am a nobody. I am not even a big nobody. I am just a nobody.

I come from a large Irish Catholic family, which in 1960 seemed to be a highly relevant thing to our nation, if not to me. I was just 6 years old and clearly recall only two things I saw on television that year -Bill Mazeroski's game seven homer against the New York Yankees and a Kennedy-Nixon debate. I don't know why Mazeroski's homer made such an impact upon me. Perhaps I had never witnessed a grown man act so much like one of us kids. In any event I'm glad I remember it, but back to the point. Nixon and Kennedy acted differently –they seemed more serious than any adult I had ever seen. Though I had no aptitude for the debate, the roomful of aunts and uncles, and distant relatives, all gathered together before my grandparent's television, signified to me something unusual was happening; something big. Now, it is important to relate that my extended family was comprised of both Republicans and Democrats, but the majority of them were independent, and tended to vote for the *"best man"* as the phrase went in those days. Politics didn't enter into that first vote I cast, but I could clearly see that this Kennedy fellow would have been my choice for president because I had no doubt he would have made a better daddy than that other guy Nixon.

DON'T VOTE FOR ME

Kennedy had nice hair, a friendly face and seemed to be capable of having fun in the fine Irish style I will always treasure. Little did I know then that from that time on politics and baseball –not necessarily always in that order– would keep me so easily entertained, even though these interests more often than not leave me needlessly annoyed.

My Grandfather Brennan was a huge influence on me in the political realm. He always watched Face the Nation or Meet the Press before or after Sunday Mass. In subsequent years ABC's *Issues and Answers* was added to the mix. The Kennedy years were great times for a young Catholic kid growing up in Port Huron. My grade school teacher, Sister Timothy, was an unabashed Kennedy supporter. On the day of his assassination she broke into tears and dismissed the students from class, unable to articulate the emergency, other than, *"Everyone needs to go home. Something terrible has happened."* On the day of Kennedy's funeral the young children in the neighborhood (we called ourselves *"The Non-Swearers Club"*) built the *John F. Kennedy Memorial Bridge* over a small crick in the woods opposite our houses on Sanborn Street. Later we constructed the *Abraham Lincoln Memorial Bridge*. I kid you not. We probably would have built bridges for all of the presidents had the crick been bigger and if winter had not been on the horizon. Looking back I now realize that we were brought up both at school and in our homes to have great pride in our country. To be perfectly honest, back then I didn't even know or care that I was of Irish ancestry. Children

DON'T VOTE FOR ME

were simply proud to be Americans and we revered our elected leaders.

As kids we were ecstatic to see Republican Governor George Romney walk in Port Huron's parade; we admired Democrat Phil Hart and Republican Bob Griffin, our U.S. Senators. It was not a perfect world by any means but there was a civility in those days that we took for granted, and we were a much better democracy for it. On those political programs at NBC, CBS, and ABC, I don't recall anything but polite discourse. When asked, a candidate could answer a reporter's question without being cut off by his adversary. In a debate each side was given the opportunity to give a free and uninterrupted answer, an answer, which was given within the strict dictates of time. It was a respectful setting. They played by the rules. No candidate would dare to exhibit the lack of class we too often witness not only in today's political climate, but everywhere in our culture. Sure serious disagreements existed. Political storms brewed on the horizon and there was strident competition to sway the American middle just like today. I'm sure some candidates took some liberties with the facts. After all politicians are politicians. But at least their efforts didn't come across as propagandistic sound bites, half truths and lies repeated *ad nauseum*, all of which we now see and hear on a constant basis. Candidates contended without being contentious. Debates were real debates, not regurgitated talking points. And believe it or not Republicans and Democrats could in those days agree to compromise for the nation's good once in a

DON'T VOTE FOR ME

while, split the difference and call it a day. But it didn't last.

Speaking for myself, the American machine started losing control in the Lyndon Johnson presidency with the intractable mess in Viet Nam, the wheels came off with the Robert F. Kennedy assassination, and the car crashed with the release of Richard Nixon's Watergate tapes. Before my 20th year I had seen one president lose not only the respect of his opposition but that of his own party, and of the entire nation; I had seen lightning strike Camelot twice and I discovered that our leaders did not so much cover up the crimes of others, but rather cover up an entirely parallel world where, behind the scenes, they employed all of the language and phraseology of drunken sailors. I was very naïve. The subsequent revelations of JFK's affairs-and so much more gossip- even extended into the world of sports as Jim Bouton's book *Ball Four* hit the bestseller list. All of these scandals added to the wreckage until finally my secular worship of sports and politics sunk in the waters below the Chappaquiddick Bridge.

My eyes were opened but my heart yearned for reclamation because I too had begun to live life contrary to good common sense to which I had once been faithful. The little Catholic boy on Sanborn Street in Port Huron had also grown up and become a full-fledged member of *"The Swearers Club."* And while I found in adulthood I could deal with the indiscretions of Teddy, Nixon, and Mantle, I was still thankful that political naivety got me to age twenty, because most kids today are contaminated by age 10. And somehow 32 years later, I found myself wondering if I could build

DON'T VOTE FOR ME

a new bridge over deeper, wider, and swifter currents of cynical waters. With that in mind, as I fast forward to life at age 52, I invite you to my world as a candidate.

DON'T VOTE FOR ME

CHAPTER II
THE SETTING

My birthday was approaching. Although I found myself in very good health, I had just seen the ravages of cancer take my sister-in-law a month earlier. She was only 46 years old when she died. She had no obvious signs of pancreatic cancer and no one had any reason to think she shouldn't have enjoyed a long healthy life. We all like to think we will have time for everything. But usually everything overwhelms us, and then we have time for nothing. Or so it seems.

On my birthday, I decided to take a hike in the woods and collect my thoughts. The words of my law school commencement speaker, Gordon Schaber, Dean of the McGeorge School of Law, haunted me. *"I am 57 years old,"* he said to us. *"You are young, but I tell you right now to appreciate how thin a sliver of time life really is. Don't take it for granted."* That quote is the only thing I remember of his speech. And there I was 20 years later, having never taken his advice. I stopped for a moment and exhaling into the cool April air, I imagined seeing time itself dispersing into a fog of broken dreams, into a mist of chances not taken.

Yes, life is a vapor. And I thought what if I blink at yet another birthday, satisfied to live life remaining on the sidelines- not to live life as I should, but to let others direct me as they would? My chosen field in life is the practice of law, and I had, as

DON'T VOTE FOR ME

many other lawyers, satisfied myself to allow others having little practical knowledge of law dominate the legislature, and in my opinion, turn the State Capitol building itself into a marketplace of biennial opportunism. And I write this with all due respect to the voters who elect these sorts of people, and to their lobbyists who write the laws that govern my practice. Let me be precise: Our elected representatives do not know the law, they do not write the law, they do not read the law and they do not work with the law. They *"sponsor"* the laws, with the absolute certainty that the lobbyist who promoted the legislation will be reminded of this sort of support in their next campaign fundraiser.

Now this way of making law is not always bad, but it is bad when it is always made in this fashion. And if this revelation comes as a shock to anyone, be comforted for now, because it is likely to get worse.

Another, perhaps more, insidious encroachment upon the state representative assembly is the progressively dictatorial federal government, which itself is also becoming less and less a representative body and more and more an administrative bureaucracy. The Feds all too often demand that the States do its bidding utilizing the power of the immense federal purse. They command us to do as *"they"* say or *"they"* won't let you share in *"their"* funding. In Money We Trust.

Finally I had come to the solid conclusion that our state's noble effort to limit the terms of elected officials, while perhaps

DON'T VOTE FOR ME

wonderful in theory, had miserably failed in practice –especially in regards to the legislative branch. In my opinion, term limits have proved to be an unmitigated disaster. There is now more power grabbing, partisanship, incompetence and distrust among our state's elected officials than ever.

All of these genuine problems remain now as they did then. I would happily endure them as a citizen and as an attorney if I had the confidence our elected leaders rise from an enlightened, involved, and informed electorate, but this is not the case. Far worse than that, we the people have become just too damn busy to assume responsibility for our role in government. Every election we are promised governmental bread and governmental circuses, which will lead us the way of the Roman Empire, and yet we whine for more.

So I decided to quit complaining, get off the sidelines and get into the game. The trouble was that it was late in the fourth quarter when I decided to enter the arena and I wasn't entirely convinced whose team I wanted to join. Admittedly, I am conservative by nature. I am center-right. I would characterize my place on the zoological chart somewhere between the endangered species of conservative Democrat and moderate Republican. From 1979-1982 I worked for the Michigan Republican Party, yet I am a registered Democrat. During the time I worked for the Michigan Republican Party, Governor Bill Milliken was a progressive pro-choice Republican, and the Party chairman was Mel Larsen, a pro-life civil rights advocate. By today's standards, those two figures

DON'T VOTE FOR ME

would not likely be so welcome in the Republican fold. Neither would John Anderson, the 1980 Republican presidential primary candidate who was probably the last Republican to present a somewhat liberal philosophy to a national audience. I will speak of Anderson later, but in any event I was not running as a liberal, but as a progressive conservative, which is a whole different political creature than a Progressive, but I was not a knee-jerk conservative either. Philosophically, I would support a good and workable idea even if it ran counter to my preferred conservative position. On the other hand, all things being equal my nature is my general guide. I am willing to be persuaded by a good and convincing argument for change, even radical change as long as the proposed solution is sound using syllogistic reasoning. Most importantly however, I would subject all proposed legislation to a strict cost-benefit analysis. Just because an idea is good does not make it affordable. Government must simply stop trying to be all things to all people, spending money which is not ours. We must be just, before we are generous. Can't both parties agree with this reasoning?

Anyhow, there I was. With just two days remaining to file for office. I knew it was now or never. There were five Republicans and two Democrats already seeking the open seat in that primary, because Scott Hummel the incumbent Republican representative was *"limited out"* by Michigan law. Simple division, as much as political persuasion, was a factor that made the decision easy for me. Plus, there was the obvious historical

DON'T VOTE FOR ME

fact that my district had never elected a Democrat State Representative, so I chose the pragmatic route and decided to run as a Republican. Immediately I lost half my friends.

Coincidentally I was due to fly with my sister to Las Vegas the Monday evening before the filing deadline of Tuesday, May 16th. My brothers and sisters had scheduled a three-day, two-night reunion months beforehand when I had no thought of running for office, and I was committed to following through with our plans. So now it was crunch time. On Monday, May 15, 2006 at precisely 4:00 PM -at the proverbial 11th hour- I checked out of the third floor Prosecutor's office and walked down one flight of stairs to the County Clerk's office to officially file. I had told no one at work of the decision I had made over the weekend to run for State Representative. As I descended the stairs I felt nervous but also proud satisfaction that I was about to leave the comfort zone for an unknown realm. I was a bit self-conscious and found myself suddenly shaking uncontrollably as I entered the Clerk's office. Worse yet, even though I saw these courthouse employees nearly every day I could neither make an intelligible sentence out of my words, nor coordinate my actions. My behavior became totally and inexplicably schizoid. To them I must have looked like I had seen a ghost.

"Uh. Hi-i-i-I, uhhh, um. I'm filing... here is my... who do I write... where is my check?" I stammered, as I was fumbling around in my shirt pocket for a pen to write the check for the filing fee. I had the foresight to bring two pens just in case one didn't

DON'T VOTE FOR ME

work, but as I pulled one out, my other pen fell to the floor. As I bent to pick that one up, I dropped the pen that was in my hand. So I picked that one up too, and then as I did, all of the paper work fell out of my other trembling hand. The clerk's floor was littered with my debris. Somewhere in the clutter was my check, as well as the other forms necessary for filing. So there I was. I had been working at the courthouse for 17 years and I was a complete mess. The clerks were stunned to mystified silence. They had absolutely no idea why I was even there, much less what accounted for my bizarre behavior.

After I collected my pen, my notebook, my papers, my check, my keys, and finally my thoughts, I blurted out, *"Okay, let me start over. I'm running for the State Rep seat. It is 100 dollars, right?"*

"Um, yes," came a sympathetic reply. *"But you don't file here Kevin. You have to file at the Secretary of State's office in Lansing."*

I was mortified. *"What?!"* I exclaimed. *"I called the Secretary of State's office and they told me to file at the County Clerk office."*

"Well, that's true, but only in Wayne County. Everywhere else it must be filed with the Secretary of State, Kevin, in Lansing. You have to file in Lansing. But," she cheerfully added, *"don't worry, you have all day tomorrow."*

DON'T VOTE FOR ME

Well, I can't tell you that bit of bad news let the air out of my balloon because it pretty well burst in the explosion of pens, papers, and keys moments before. But now things weren't just embarrassing, this was a real crisis. Now I had but one hour to make it to downtown Lansing, which is ordinarily a simple task to be sure, but then so is taking a pen out of one's pocket. Besides that, I still had to pick up my sister so we could to make it to Detroit on time for our flight to Vegas. There was a real chance I wouldn't be filing after all. Even so, I felt a strange peace within. I had **tried**, damn it. I tried. No one could say I didn't! I didn't back down. I didn't give in to cowardice. If I couldn't make it to Lansing in time to file, well then let it be said that I got knocked out on a technicality, on a miscommunication. There is no sin in that. No shame. I had invested nothing but the decision to run and if my chance didn't come to fruition now, there would always be another time. Hold your head high, Kevin. The drop of a pen had finally broken the ice of an age. I had taken a step; maybe just one, but this citizen had taken a stand...well, sort of. Okay, maybe I was on hands and knees picking up debris, but symbolism counts in politics.

So very calmly, realizing the all in all, I responded, *"Well, I can't do it tomorrow because I have to catch a plane for Las Vegas in Detroit. So if I don't make it to Lansing before 5:00 PM I'll just run next time."* I can't say my promise compared in degree or kind, but I was in the mind of General Douglas MacArthur.

I quickly thanked them for their advice and departed in

DON'T VOTE FOR ME

benign resignation. So there I was. What a start. It's funny. You set out to represent nearly 100,000 people and it begins like it's the loneliest journey of all. In the end the *"gods"* were with me. My sister was ready to go and we made it to the Secretary of State office in Lansing without a hitch, well before closing.

I was surprised to find that only one other filer was present -a short blond guy wearing spectacles filing for a seat in Genesee County. He was shorter than me and I'm only 5'8" on a good day twenty years ago. I got the impression he was an incumbent. He strutted around their offices like he was the cock of the walk, and made damn sure they had better damn well know he was pretty damn important. It wasn't hard to tell a guy like him would have been hard to work with. He was rude and officious to the state's civil servants who were unnecessarily polite, competent, and pleasant to him in response. I wondered how a guy like that could ever be elected. Apparently his voters never got to see how he really acted in Lansing.

Anyhow, my behavior in Lansing projected far more confidence than the debacle at the county clerk's office. I was calm and polite and things went smoothly. And by way of contrast to that other guy from Flint, I was like a knight in shining armor.

In a flash my papers were stamped and my life had forever changed. *Finally!* Now I was a candidate! It was a breeze, and within moments I was back in the car with my sister. We were off to Nevada where I would spend the first night of my campaign.

DON'T VOTE FOR ME

Soon we were on a plane full of happy faces, Vegas-bound, where everything is possible, even if the odds are always 100,000 to one.

DON'T VOTE FOR ME

CHAPTER III
A WICKED START

I didn't know how a trip to Vegas would impact my campaign. I suspected some would consider it negatively for religious or for other moral reasons. As for me, I've been to Vegas three times in my life and I've enjoyed its unique contribution to things Americana. I am not offended by the ordinary venial frivolity one can experience there, and besides, there is little happening in Las Vegas that can't be seen during television family hour on network television.

That doesn't make everything that happens there acceptable, but it is a fact. Undoubtedly one can more easily cross over into the grayer side of things such as excessive gambling, drinking, and perverse fornications, but unless you're predisposed to such diversions, you are likely to fly home in a state of grace notwithstanding. But on the other hand, isn't it one's glory to watch the sunrise along the strip after a night of experiencing a most spectacular metamorphosis of that culture of profligate living? That is a highly relevant question because we arrived so late at night in Vegas and that is exactly what I experienced. That night my brother and I stayed up the entire first night.

After a quick blast downtown with my siblings, we made the fateful decision to take the last monorail back to the strip. By the time we got there it was nearly 3:00 AM with no monorail to

DON'T VOTE FOR ME

take us back to the Hilton. So we spent the night on the strip reconfirming the laws of probability, re-learning phrases like house advantage and remembering why I so infrequently gamble. But as the hours passed and the homeless began to seek refuge like bats at daybreak, my brother and I decided rather than waste good slot machine money on a cab we would hike all the way back to the Hilton. All I could think was, *"Wow, it's been a long time since I've stayed up all night... moron!"* But it wouldn't be long until I would do it again, and again, and again.

And so there I was. Absolutely and totally exhausted. This was the start of my campaign. The next day, well, not the next day, but the same day I was already in, separated by a fitful hour or two's spell of rest, I re-joined my wiser relatives who were hanging out by the hotel pool. I was dog-tired and was no longer that happy face on the plane from Detroit. For most of the day my brother-in-law kept insisting in his sober and clipped South African accent that I was crazy to run for office and must opt out of the situation before the real cost of running was realized. Worst of all, in my compromised and weakened condition I knew he was making sense with his points. You have no plan. You're relying on luck. What you are doing amounts to a long-shot gamble. And by the way, how did it go last night?

Just the day before in Michigan, I had no doubt I was on the right path. After just one night in Vegas with my energy sapped, reasonable, rational doubt crept in. I was already losing confidence. Back home the odds- just like in Vegas- were against

DON'T VOTE FOR ME

my success. I could say a lot more about my Las Vegas time and adventures, but first I'll have to run it by Mayor Goodman, so I'll leave those details for my book tour. Okay, so I peeked at the Elvis statue at the Hilton before its official unveiling. So sue me.

Wednesday turned into Thursday on the flight home as I spent another sleepless night -the second in three days- jetting back to Michigan. I was now ten times more exhausted than I was forty-eight hours earlier. The three day, one night Vegas remedy, sandwiched between two red-eye flights left me a caffeinated zombie. I was REM deprived, and I had to work the morning I returned. Worst of all, I had told no one at the office about running for State Representative. Of course, after Monday's red kryptonite behavior at the County Clerk's office I was absolutely certain word of it had spread throughout the courthouse during my three-day hiatus like the gossip of a frustrated popinjay, thank you Bill O'Reilly. And sure enough it had, as it should have.

So there I was, back at work, as though I had just completed an ultra-marathon. I was entirely phobic of stares, glances, and low-toned conversations that I interpreted as negative aspersions being all about me. How could it be otherwise? I knew it would happen! But I knew darn well I would have reacted no differently than they if the shoe had been on the other foot. Being grumpy and sleep deprived I just couldn't muster the requisite desire to address their natural curiosity about my decision to run. I knew they deserved at least a scripted explanation on my part but I was churlish and defensive and reacted to their inquisition like a

DON'T VOTE FOR ME

sick, wounded, and tired animal. Foremost in my mind was an escape route. I just wanted to retreat to my den, sleep, and regroup. When my boss asked me about my big surprise, if it was true I had really filed, I responded with a standoffish surly non-answer akin to *"yeah so far it's true."* By law I had seven days to withdraw from the race without penalty, so I wanted people to know I was thinking about that so I could get through the day without presenting myself in a phony *"Hey! Let's be positive about me as a candidate!"* mode. I would have hated myself for acting that way, not that I was emanating vibrations of joy otherwise. I felt isolated and spent. I could not justify my decision to run.

All in all, it was clear that going to Las Vegas was a huge mistake. Maybe coming home was a bigger one! On the other hand, and from another perspective, I was kind of proud that I hadn't become like so many of the other candidates who had already started living 24/7 sucking up to the public. But I was living 24/7, literally. I just wasn't living a politically correct lifestyle.

In the next three days, it would only get way, way, way more disproportionate in that regard -yes, unbelievably so. Early, very early the very next day I was off for yet another three-day test of endurance -this time on my son's middle school field trip to Chicago. So after I got off the plane from Las Vegas I drove two hours back to St. Johns, worked all day, and then got up at 4:00 AM Friday, just in time to get on a bus with fifty 8th graders for a slow bus trip to the city with broad shoulders. In the end, three

DON'T VOTE FOR ME

more precious days were wasted from a candidate's perspective.

Curiously, my biggest political gaffe resulted from my review of the musical *Wicked*, which was playing at the Ford Oriental Theatre. It was the capstone of the class trip. The teacher who coordinated the entire field trip asked me in a very pleasant voice how I liked the musical. Unaware of her opinion, I, ever the sentimental traditionalist responded with undaunted assertiveness just how awful I thought the play was. Encapsulating my review, I boldly opined it was an unoriginal rip off of a classic piece of American theater, with a message designed to entice those left brain thinkers whose inclinations are to fancifully believe that they can always somehow find unwarranted justification for their own bad behavior.

As a politician I should have realized my obtuse right-wing review of *Wicked* meant absolutely nothing to the teacher and the bigger goal of getting her vote had been forever lost. A politician can sometimes differ with a voter on the issues and still get his or her vote, but once you run afoul of their feelings or something politically irrelevant but personal to them, trust me, you can kiss their support goodbye forever. Worse, you made a political enemy! If I was to gain her vote, here is what I should have said. I should have asked, *"How did you like it?"* And after I had discovered her rave review, answered her question a bit more diplomatically with something like, *"What a shame to be born green and ugly, especially when she had such a beautiful sister. It explains everything. It has given me a whole new perspective on*

19

DON'T VOTE FOR ME

her behavior in the Wizard of Oz." Of course it would have been less than honest, but at least that answer wouldn't have offended her. How stupid could I have been to think that she would have agreed with my negative review? The focal point of her entire three-day field trip to Chicago was attending that play. How could I have been so, well, so much like a man!?

Later that same ride home, realizing my lack of diplomacy, I wised up and tried to un-ring the bell. I assured her that my opinion was a minority view, that the kids -especially my own son really liked it. And maybe later when I had time to think it over I might change my mind too. But it was all BS pure and simple. I was just saying it to remove an obstacle if she might later learn that I was a candidate for office. How trite was that? So there I was- crying, pleading, groveling for forgiveness, understanding, and acceptance...just like the Wicked Witch of the West in *Wicked.* If the late Chicagoan Paul Harvey could have commentated on my sad behavior, he would have concluded his report with his patented sigh of condescending disgust, *"Ah, humm..."*

Anyhow, the bus trip was far from over. I pondered over the next several weeks of my life. And the more I pondered I realized I just didn't have the fire in the belly to do that kind of cajoling, apologizing, mitigating, and obfuscating. I didn't do any campaigning on the bus tour, although there was ample opportunity. There were about twenty adults on the trip, but only one of them knew I was running for office. I chatted with her for a while about some of the things going on in Michigan. As with my

DON'T VOTE FOR ME

South African brother-in-law the more she quizzed me on my immediate political future the more starkly reality stared me in the face. The same themes were repeated. I had no campaign strategy, but everyone else did. I did not have a staff, or a contact person. I had not solicited endorsements. I had no money. I had no plan. Most of all, however, I discovered that I lacked the will to live, breathe, eat, sleep, and walk and talk as a missionary of self promotion, disguised as a passionate zealot for the masses. Politicians have little choice but to become superficial, artificial babbling entities to a very large extent. Think about it. Voters say they want our opinions, but we do not dare offend anyone on any subject, whether intended or not, whether misquoted or not. It is just the way it is. And it has become that way because we let it, demand it, or both.

Nevertheless, I told her that all my deficiencies could be rectified once I squared off against my opponents in debates. Ah, the debates -like Kennedy and Nixon! I hoped with adequate and fair press coverage, the mystical, informed, involved and responsible electorate would give me the fair, honest assessment I would most certainly need. I was going to be the politician to break the mold. I knew I had no other chance. As the school bus rolled into the St. Johns Middle School parking lot on that Sunday sunrise, I clung to that one single affirmation.

And for the first time in my campaign I slept peaceably well into the afternoon, dreaming of flying scarecrows and tin monkeys.

DON'T VOTE FOR ME

CHAPTER IV

THE DOMESTIC CAMPAIGN BEGINS

Memorial weekend ushered in the biggest single event of my district in the course of the campaign -the Alma Highland Festival. It celebrates Scots heritage and it is indeed a Celtic spectacular. Bagpipes and reunions of Scottish clans, market stalls and athletic events punctuate the activities, but the place to be seen was the Highland Parade. Luckily for me, the event organizers barred candidates from participation in the parade – a condition I welcomed as I had but two cheap *"Hayes for State Representative"* tee-shirts with ironed-on patches in my entire campaign inventory. I had no literature, pamphlets, brochures or signs. I had my bicycle, my tee-shirt and me. That was it.

Though prohibited from parading, candidates were allowed to go to the festival itself, so I drove up to Alma with my mountain bike atop my yellow 2002 Aztec. The parade was just winding up as I arrived downtown. I was able to find a parking spot next to City Hall. As I readied my bike for the ride over to Alma College where the Highland events were happening, a thin talkative man about my age saw my tee-shirt and began to engage in conversation with me. He was a Republican and a bike enthusiast. He had kind words about George Bush, which was rarely heard that summer anywhere. He asked if I was a pro-life candidate. For a moment, I hesitated. I did not want my candidacy to be defined by that issue, especially since the legal reality is that nothing can

22

DON'T VOTE FOR ME

be done about it unless *Roe v. Wade* is overturned, or until there is an amendment to the U.S. Constitution. But the subject was unavoidable. I knew it.

In my very first vote as an 18 year old in 1972, I joined the overwhelming majority of Michigan citizens opposing a legislative initiative to liberalize Michigan's pre-*Roe v. Wade* statute. That law from 1931 is still on the books, but remains unenforceable under *Roe*. It is a simple and succinct stature, which proscribes anyone, including, licensed medical professionals from performing abortions, except in those cases in which the mother's life in endangered. In any event, having learned from the *Wicked* fiasco, I responded, *"I am."* And I had my first supporter. As we parted he gave me his business card, and I happily pedaled west down Main Street. It was short-lived bliss. To my amazement before me marched armies and legions of workers from my opponents' campaigns! Their literature and brochures littered the streets. It was clear that the ban of political campaigning had been violated big-time. I was livid! I had no representation in the parade, and rather than be credited by the citizens of Alma for abiding by their rules, I surmised the opposite would result; I would be maligned for not caring enough to participate in it! Well, I was there, following the rules, but so what? I locked my bike and walked dejectedly to the festival grounds. I couldn't help but think that the very men who would have us live under the law seemed to think every rule is a suggestion when it applies to them. Well, at least the rules didn't preclude me from wearing my tee-shirt with the

23

DON'T VOTE FOR ME

iron-on patch, but no one seemed to care or notice anyhow. I would have gained more attention if instead my shirt proclaimed: *"I am an Orthodox Druid."*

As luck would have it I ran into a long-lost friend of Scots heritage, a Republican from the Bill Milliken-Mel Larsen days who was home temporarily from a work assignment in Germany. We reminisced over a beer and headed over to the athletic field where they were conducting a strongman contest called *"The Farmers Walk."* It required that contestants lift and carry 400 pounds of welded iron rail sections as far as possible around an oval track. I attempted to pick up the pair of 200 pound iron pigs and after I discovered that I could do so, I entered the event. Why not? I was easily the oldest guy among the nine entrants. My goal was to go ten paces, about thirty feet. I surpassed my goal, being able to lug the bars twenty paces before setting them down. The last thing I needed was to throw out my back. I didn't go very far, but I didn't shame myself and a few spectators seemed impressed by the old guy's effort. Even though the announcer didn't mention anything about me, my campaign tee-shirt, or my candidacy to the 200 or so people who watched, it was fun anyhow. George Plimpton would have been proud of me. Unfortunately it was nothing more than an exercise in self-fulfillment. No votes rained down upon me in Alma. It just wasn't going to be that easy.

In contrast to Alma's festival, there was a somber Memorial Day parade on Tuesday, May 30th, in St. Johns. Only a couple of candidates campaigned in that parade. I thought it would

DON'T VOTE FOR ME

be offensive to try to promote myself politically on a day that is set aside to honor the ones who gave all, in service to our freedoms, but I did go to the parade as a spectator. Shamefully I admit I have seen few of these events in my life. Eventually, the small but dignified parade culminated at a ceremony at St. Johns Mount Rest Cemetery. Though the parade itself was sparse in number, I was stunned to see a huge number of people waiting there for the small parade to arrive. I was humbled by their attendance. It is not so much that I didn't know my community consisted of good Americans -I was sure of that beforehand. I was just amazed that so many came out on a rather brisk, gray day with thunder and rain approaching from the west. I stood way in the back. I struggled with a sense of hypocrisy. I never joined. I never served. I never sacrificed. I was a politician, not a soldier.

I listened to State Senator Alan Cropsey give an excellent speech. Alan is quite conservative, but so is his district. He was our long-time Republican state senator and before that, our state representative. He is a good man all around, and now he is out of office because of term limits. Why? It is ridiculous. He is still relatively young, and his decades of experience, skill, and effectiveness are now relegated to history. We will not be a better State for losing his honesty, knowledge, and competence.

The people in the assembly honored those who had died or suffered serving our nation -right or wrong, left or right, Democrat or Republican, black or white. But I wondered to myself, do soldiers serve to protect my political aspirations? Who were they

DON'T VOTE FOR ME

and what were they serving? The rights of the pornographer down the highway? The preacher raising money on cable TV? We presume to say they are, but I don't think so. I think many serve because they signed up to do a job, and it is only later that they come to understand that their efforts produce and protect the rights envisioned by our Founding Fathers. Above all, I think they submit to this higher calling to protect their comrades, their brothers and sisters who learn to think and live with that same discipline and pride, and who will die if necessary under the warrior ethos. Our soldiers have risen far above our insistence as civilians to live a spoiled, selfish lifestyle based upon rights.

As I walked away from the cemetery, I had the sense of having done very little for my country. Could running for office change that feeling? Was I worthy? Everything I had done my first week of campaigning was campaign neutral, at best. I secured one vote. By the weekend, I was feeling pretty sorry for myself. To say that I discovered that the majority of people are apathetic is an extreme understatement. The overwhelming majority is too apathetic to even appreciate that they are apathetic. They don't even care enough to care about voting in a primary!

I was finding out very quickly that my late filing and slow but righteous pace caused me to fall further and further behind. In addition to the head start my opponents had due to my late entry, they were adding more voters each week than I was. And if the fault wasn't my message, then as a candidate the blame was mine alone. I couldn't *"work a crowd."* I didn't feel comfortable

DON'T VOTE FOR ME

making small talk and backslapping strangers. It wasn't in my nature to interject myself into someone's life. I had no desire to hoodwink, bamboozle or give them the ol' okie-dokie.

Although my family was supportive, I was embarrassed by the lack of interest and enthusiasm I was experiencing. I wasn't feeling the love. I wasn't getting good vibes from people who didn't know me from Adam. I saw how much ground I would have to cover in a short period to make a respectable showing. I knew it would require an inordinate amount of time -time I didn't want to sacrifice. I alone among the six Republican candidates had to work full time. How could I compete? Besides, I had a decent job with an average income for my education. I didn't need to be a politician.

Well, I had one hundred other good, solid reasons to get out but little did I know what the next few days would bring. Oh Lordy, suddenly, praise be to God, manna from heaven fell like monsoon rains! Oh did it ever! All of a sudden I was deluged with dozens -I dare say- well over one hundred requests for my views on a variety of issues and the accompanying lure of possible political support! First only a letter or two per day arrived in my post office box. But soon it multiplied into five or six or more per day until soon it became clear I would never have the time to respond to all of these informed citizens. It seemed that I had finally found a surefire way of getting my message out without spending money I didn't have! I could become known! The fuse was ready to be lit! The cavalry had arrived! I poured over letter

DON'T VOTE FOR ME

after letter. Some were so gracious as to enclose a return envelope and even prepare a questionnaire addressing the issues important to them. Others invited me to meet with them to discuss my political views. When the letters first arrived I quickly responded. I answered the questions, and gladly adjusted my schedule to fit theirs. I was intrigued and enticed. It was just like the early days of internet email and scams, where one was promised wealth and affection from strangers all over the globe. How come I was receiving this manna from heaven? Who were these angelic messengers of hope and change? And why were they suddenly so interested in me and my one-man campaign? Where had they been up until now? Finally their fawning adulation and solicitation led up to the greatest interview I had ever given. At least that is what I thought.

Gongwer News telephoned all of the candidates to get a take on the issues in that particular election cycle ~the economy, affirmative action, taxation, and gay marriage among them. I conversed with the reporter for twenty minutes and my answers rolled off my tongue like golden Cadillacs cruising Woodward Avenue on a hot summer night back in the day. Somehow everything clicked, and I delivered my words in an unrehearsed, smooth, polished and finished product ready to drive home.

In my discourse with the reporter my points were simple. The economy is bad for a variety of reasons, I said. But the problems will never be solved by the legislature and local units of government habitually enticing manufacturers with tax breaks and

DON'T VOTE FOR ME

credits on a discriminatory case by case basis. The state's failure to generate a real business plan was compounded by a brain drain from Michigan. Though the governor and legislature usually increased revenues for higher education so that the corporate world could avail itself of learned graduates, our best and brightest had learned one thing from our state above all: it is in their best interest to leave the state and to work and reside in places other than Michigan where state governments have figured out we are in the 21st century now, not the 1900's. Poll after poll confirmed that our youth had no faith in Michigan's immediate future and having no faith in our future, there was no power in the present.

My position on affirmative action was an easy call. To me the most insidious and pernicious result of the civil rights movement was the ridiculous notion that equal protection under the law could come into balance by state-sanctioned bigotry. Worse, those who benefit by such policies seemed completely oblivious to an acceptable way to bring an end to this "lawful" discrimination. How can it be that a nation which is so steeped and current in prejudice and racial avarice that a person of "minority" heritage should be able to receive extra credit for that status by this same damnable government? Why are so many immigrants from Africa and Mexico, from the Caribbean and from all of Latin America busting down our doors to get in? Indeed, even Muslims seek refuge here, leaving their own lands to come to this awful place so full of sin, hate and prejudice.

I gave an anecdotal example of my angst. The State Bar of

DON'T VOTE FOR ME

Michigan, the sanctioning authority for the licensing of attorneys only recently abandoned their stupid notion *"that in order to promote a bias-free organization, [that you] please voluntarily disclose [your] racial identity."* In the beginning they listed four options: white, black, Hispanic, and *"other."* Later they tried to make us lawyers more bias-free by dividing our choices to further include Arab-American, Pacific Islanders, or gay/lesbian. Finally, as they became more and more successful in unifying our profession by annually subdividing us further, they added the off the charts category that collapsed the whole counter-intuitive absurdity under its own weight. They wanted to know how many of us might classify ourselves as *"transgender."*

I was insulted by these questions. I admit that I may have checked the box "white" early in my career due to the prospect that Big Brother might come down on me for not voluntarily helping to promote a "bias-free organization", but simple, syllogistic reasoning led me to the utterly inescapable conclusion that answering that question could and would lead to everything but a bias-free organization. Is the NBA biased because only a few of its players may be able to check some box white, Asian or Hispanic? It was clear the State Bar was really interested in using such information only so that it could be said one glorious day far into our future that our profession had finally reached a point at which we could proclaim ourselves bias free, or proportionally politically correct, or something. God knows they were really doing the work of conservatives, because at the rate they were

DON'T VOTE FOR ME

creating new options to check off they were sure to establish a category unique for each one of its members!

In any event, I surmised that since the State Bar couldn't figure out that if I was *"white"* in 1987, and that I probably would still be white in 1988, I began to doubt it myself. And finally it dawned on me who and what God made me. I was just like everyone else -except perhaps Dennis Kucinich. An epiphany came over me. My true genesis and place in the universe was just this: I was always -and became henceforth forevermore in this life –something more discernable than just an "other." I discovered my true identity- I was an *"Earthling,"* and with that I gave the State Bar a new category to contemplate. And then glory be to God, the State Bar stopped asking all of us those insane questions.

I expounded briefly on the issue of gay marriage. For my part, while I could not linguistically or religiously define or condone the concept as being equal in all respects to traditional marriage as many in the gay community advocate, in a secular legal sense, which is the domain of the legislature and not the church, I would not oppose civil unions. I am not blind to the fact that there are gay churches, which are performing such rites without legislative approval; I cannot deny them that right. But I cannot say it is right.

My position regarding un-tabulated self-authenticating *"immigration"* was plain and simple. We should love our neighbors, but they don't get to come into the house without

DON'T VOTE FOR ME

permission. That is trespassing. If they get permission, it does not mean they can do as they wish. They are guests. They don't get to come in, have babies, and then insist that they are now part of the family, except by house rules. I'm sure our teachers had it all wrong back in the 1960's, but when we were all singing *"This Land is Your Land,"* they taught us that Woody Guthrie was referring to America and Americans, not to everyone on the planet who boldly demands the right to come and stay here on their own accord. We just can't let everyone in. After all, look at all that has happened since 1492!

Maybe my thesis was influenced by my belief in UFO's. I sometimes wonder how we can justify so much insane public policy. What would Martians think of our line of reasoning? Anyhow, after my blast-off into the unknown, Gongwer finally managed to remind me I was off the ground only as high as a telephonic soapbox, and I was able to parachute safely back down to good mother Earth.

DON'T VOTE FOR ME

CHAPTER V
I CAN'T GET OUT!

Anyhow, speaking of Earth, it was taking a pounding. One candidate, Mike Trebesh, had his signs up around the countryside for nearly a year, but now in early June, Paul Opsommer's signs were mushrooming everywhere.

I was stunned by the timing and by the quantity and quality of signs that appeared. It was overwhelming. The signs appeared in all shapes and sizes throughout the most populous part of the district in southern Clinton County. Entire neighborhoods in Dewitt were laced with them. Opsommer's campaign was laying out some big, big dollars -dollars I neither had nor would be able to raise. His tour de force was a resounding message, a full frontal attack. Clearly, Opsommer had plenty of money, visibility, and organization. He had a base, but most of all he had a plan, and it was a plan that was long in the making. It was another reality check, one more cold slap in the face.

I was badly outflanked, vastly outnumbered, and I hadn't even met my opponents in person yet, though I had spoken to Republican hopeful Josh Nunez over the phone right after an old friend of mine called me on his behalf. Although I can't recall my friend's exact words, my memory is sharp and clear enough to present an accurate if not exact reiteration. He told me I had to drop out of the campaign because I had no chance of winning.

DON'T VOTE FOR ME

That Josh Nunez would definitely win. That going forward would bring unnecessary calamity to my life and my family. Okay, he didn't use the word calamity, but that was the gist of it. Now these admonitions were not threats from an enemy -they were said to me as advice coming from a friend. He was earnest in his conviction that I needed to get out now. That conversation lasted for a while. It was his dime anyhow. He went on. Josh Nunez was a great looking guy. He was extremely bright and articulate. He was young and charismatic. He was politically connected and most important of all was his capture of the district's Christian fundamentalist vote. *"It's too late, Kevin,"* he said. *"You should have told me you were running. You know I would have helped. You're a great guy. You would have made a great legislator, but..."*

I replied: *"So just tell Josh to drop out and have him support me instead."*

He was quick to respond that he couldn't do that, which was followed by more blah, blah, blah.

So there I was, the heathen Catholic, determined to remain a secular candidate insofar as possible. In good Biblical form I told him that I would find sheep of my own. I'll not steal or even try to dissuade any of Josh's supporters or anyone else's for that matter. I would have to find my own voters. And in retrospect, I can say I honored that commitment all throughout the campaign. Perhaps that commitment proved to be a political mistake, but it

DON'T VOTE FOR ME

simplified things.

Josh Nunez called me soon after that conversation. Josh was polite, though somewhat miffed that I would want to *"split"* the presumptive Christian vote between us. I reiterated to Josh that I wouldn't do that. I told him that I would not campaign upon a religious theme whatsoever, and was not about to go give born-again testimony to every pastor and his or her congregation throughout the district in order to establish my credentials. It was not that I objected to religious involvement in the political world. Thanks be to God for it. But I grew up distinctly aware of the minority status of Catholicism as a child. I've always believed the path that Kennedy blazed for Catholics was not a religious pilgrimage. Politicians have very different ministries than priests, ministers, rabbis, imams, or gurus and I don't believe the government's mission is to save souls. That is the last place we should hope to find salvation! Good God, help me if I'm wrong on this!

I had barely hung up the phone when yet another Republican operative touched base with me. This man is every politicians dream supporter. He was hardworking, aggressive, and extremely savvy in the science of coordinating and winning campaigns. He said many of the same things to me that I had already heard -don't hurt yourself by going on. That his candidate, Paul Opsommer, was well on his way to becoming a solid figure with the Christian Republicans, which I interpreted to ostensibly mean Baptist fundamentalists.

DON'T VOTE FOR ME

"But I heard Paul is a Catholic," I responded.

"Yes, that's true," he admitted. *"But lately Paul has been attending our Bible studies with my pastor and it is looking like he is coming to believe...."*

I felt like saying it took Catholics nearly 200 years to become politically acceptable in America, and I wasn't about to look back now, but it would have gone nowhere. That probably wasn't his point anyhow, but for a long time now this needless tension has permeated the Republican Party, if not Christendom itself.

These conversations culminated in the dark night of my political soul. The Republican primary -at least in these parts- is won by those with one part ability, two parts name recognition, three parts connections, five parts money, ten parts organization and one thousand parts Right to Life endorsement. The Michigan Right to Life lobby is the 800-pound gorilla in Republican politics, not unlike the 800-pound pro-choice Democratic gorilla. A candidate's position on the single issue of abortion is often determinative of primary success in both parties.

Let me digress just for one moment. Do you recall all those letters I was getting? Well, it is time to let the big cat out of the bag. Not a single damn one of them came from a citizen. Not a single damn one came from even one voter from my district! Every, I mean every, single one came from a special interest group

DON'T VOTE FOR ME

and their lobbyists.

Chief among them was the Michigan Right to Life Political Action Committee. From moment one, I had minimal desire to pursue the issue of abortion in this election, but not because it is unimportant to me or to this district. As I've earlier stated, if anyone bothered to research the issue they would know and admit that Michigan already has a statute governing the issue of abortion, should *Roe* be overturned. My opponents had no clue about that statute. Instead everything is political, and not real. I have no use for the pro-choice movement either, but I didn't want to respond to the Right to Life questionnaire. I was just not the person to carry their torch. So for a brief time I lived with the fantasy I could avoid dealing with Michigan Right to Life, but I couldn't. I wish I would have. Although there are tens of thousands fine, holy, and saintly people in that organization, I'll have nothing to do with the hierarchy of that organization ever again. To my campaign and to most of my colleagues, they proved to be just another pernicious lobbying firm with a leadership driven by all the trappings of money, power, politics, and influence peddling. Worse, their single-issue focus allows them the ability to anoint the winner of Republican primaries in districts like mine. I hazard to guess the same is true of the pro-choice lobby for Democrats. In any event here is my story:

I received a personal phone call from a Michigan RTL representative who alerted me that I would be receiving their questionnaire within a day or two and that it was imperative that I

DON'T VOTE FOR ME

completely fill it out and return it to her within the week, so that RTL could determine their need to endorse a candidate in the GOP primary. Most importantly, she made it clear that if all six of us Republicans were deemed pro-life candidates then RTL would refrain from endorsing any one of us and would not get involved in our race.

    I thought very, very, very seriously of not responding to RTL's questionnaire at all. Too many people think RTL has some mystical power to ex-communicate you from the pro-life cause, or even bar you from heaven itself, just because you do not profess the creed of their political agenda. To be sure I have my faults. I am a lawyer. A sinner. I am not Mother Teresa. If her words on the matter will not resonate spiritually with the Western world, there is little hope that mine as a politician would either. I decided to let the initial deadline pass without my participation. My views were on my website. That was all anyone needed to know, but as RTL persisted, and upon the advice and recommendations of several local elected leaders, I relented and mailed in my response. Now that I had sufficiently genuflected before Michigan RTL, I assumed that our collective pro-life philosophy would complete their review, and RTL's neutrality in our primary would be ensured. All six of us would campaign on a level playing field, or so I thought.

    As it turned out, Michigan Right to Life apparently was not satisfied with our responses to their questionnaire. They requested the physical presence of the six of us to appear before a panel of

DON'T VOTE FOR ME

RTL *"judges,"* ostensibly for the purpose of determining our orthodoxy to their cause. So when my oral exam was given, I emphasized my feeling that until *Roe* v. *Wade* is reversed there is little a state legislature can do in reality. Most importantly, when and if that day comes, Michigan's prior law would presumably be revived. I was supportive of that outcome, especially because the Michigan electorate through their rejection of the 1972 legislative initiative essentially affirmed that law. In other words, the voters had spoken, and though it originated as a Depression-era statute, let the new generation find a new consensus, if politically possible. My guess was that neither the pro-life nor pro-choice lobbies could ever muster a majority of today's voters to their polarized positions.

I can't say for sure, but perhaps that realistic assessment of things wasn't what they wanted to hear, because I never got answers to the questions I raised with them afterwards. All I know is that the Michigan RTL secretly convened to assess the positions of the six of us, and what happened next stunned the field of primary candidates. Michigan RTL adjudicated one of the six of us as *"pro-choice."* There were five extremely upset Republican candidates as a result. Worst of all, Michigan RTL refused to name which one of us was not pro-life. Believe me I pressured them intensively because I suspected it was me they deemed pro-choice. I was more than willing to go to war over it. Was it because I ardently refused to include the victim of rape in the pro-life matrix? In spite of everything how could I in my private or

DON'T VOTE FOR ME

public life require a woman to bear the child of a man who forcibly raped her? How could someone like me on a jury cast the first stone against her? Any trial would be a complete waste of time and nobody would come away a better soul or citizen by it.

As a person of reason, I am obligated to understand mitigation -the degrees, the causes, circumstances, and conditions in formulating sanctions and penalties for behavior proscribed by law. Yet the other pro-life candidates never addressed this continuum, at least not in public. It was all or nothing, and nobody in the race but me, the lawyer, even bothered to point out degrees of culpability or mitigation in this regard. As far as I could tell, the rest of the field silently endorsed what Josh Nunez constantly said throughout the campaign: that abortion is murder. I alone being the sole practicing lawyer among the group seemed to understand what that meant -that by his definition every abortion, in every circumstance, being premeditated, is murder in the first degree. That would mean that everyone involved in the act of abortion would be subject to a penalty of life without parole! So in the extreme case of forcible rape, the victim would defend herself from a life offense, while the rapist would get at most fifteen years? *C'mon!* Yes, you can argue rightfully the fetus is an innocent life, but do you really think that a prosecutor will win a case with those facts? Maybe I was just paranoid and there was a closet pro-choice candidate in the field, but I knew that was highly unlikely given everyone's public position on the issue. Anyhow the Michigan RTL never released its findings, but their decision

DON'T VOTE FOR ME

freed them to endorse a candidate for the 93rd District Republican Primary.

On Monday, June 19, the Michigan Right to Life Political Action Committee threw their considerable tonnage behind Paul Opsommer. After that 9.0 earthquake, the Republican primary election for all intents and purposes was settled.

It was then I absolutely determined, once and for all, it was time to drop out of the race and quit before I began to throw good money after bad. I announced my decision to my wife, hoping for a mutually sympathetic resignation due to circumstances beyond my control. Up to that point, we still hadn't put a great deal of money or time into the matter.

To put it mildly, my wife did not agree with my analysis. And she let me have it in no uncertain terms. It would have been better had I danced through a hive of killer bees. She dutifully informed me that she had already told everyone in her inner circle about my candidacy. She had also called and scheduled an appearance in every parade between Alma and St. Johns, Westphalia and Elsie. She had contacted friends, teachers and civic groups, and on it went for about five minutes. Though I was already well past the point of a technical knock-out, I still wasn't about to concede the fight. To my credit, my will, my reason, and my sense of self compelled me to remain standing even though she had me up against the ropes, pummeling me with unreturned verbal hammer blows. *Good Jesus,* I thought, *where does such*

DON'T VOTE FOR ME

spousal power emanate from? In spite of it all I managed one final answer to her onslaught.

"I am going to get my ass kicked! I've been out there already and people don't know me and don't care! And there's not enough time to change that! And even if there was, I'd have to do things I won't do and spend money I don't have!" There was no quit in my quit either--not yet!

Then I found out what most husbands are habitually oblivious to, and powerless to do anything about -their wives ability to stimulate the economy without any government programs. My wife had been shopping. She had already ordered brochures. She had already ordered custom stenciling for large plywood signs. No, not spending the couple hundred more I would per chance someday make in the State Legislature if successful. No. It was more like a couple thousand that I didn't have!

Righteously indignant, bloody and weak, I appealed to a non-existent referee, exclaiming, *"What?! I told you from day one that no matter what, I would only put $500 into this! That I wasn't going to penalize you or the family and put us into more debt. You know I told you that! This wasn't worth more than that to me!"*

"Oh, so it's all about you," she countered. *It's all about you isn't it?! It's always all about you. Well you have no idea –no idea how much I have done! How much others have done! How much the kids have put into this!"* And then came the Mary Todd

DON'T VOTE FOR ME

Lincoln moment, the wind milling uppercut, the deciding blow, and the knockout punch. Her final flurry of sixteen words, with its implied threat of the eternal loss of consortium and all that results from the certain execution of the same, laid me out once and for all. I fully understood that I had arrived at the point of no return. She declared:

"You don't want to know what I will do to you if you drop out now!"

And that one single line is the only reason -the only reason- I have this story to tell. That is the one and only reason why I did not quit. I did not dare to find out exactly what that meant, but I had a darn good guess. I have to tell you that it doesn't feel very good to pick yourself up from the canvas after a walloping like that. *No mas.* You win, I give up. The issue of staying in the race was over. I wasn't about to go back down for another count. So ladies and gentlemen, let the record reflect that the decision to continue my campaign had nothing to do with saving the world. It was about saving the family jewels.

43

DON'T VOTE FOR ME

CHAPTER VI

MATTHEW 26:74

On the outside I capitulated, but inside my ego needed soothing. I had to defuse for the day. I knew I would come in last place. At the end of it all, I would have to suffer all the behind-the-back talk that comes with it. I would have to endure the gossipmongers, who would bask in the slop of rumor and innuendo. For therapy I immediately began to number the days, and resolved to do penance as if this period of time was a politically secular Lenten mission. As I circled day number one, it might as well have been the start of Mardi Gras in June.

In a bizarre turn of events, I was summoned to attend a bachelor party the very day after the bout with my wife, and she encouraged me to go. Still badly bruised, battered, sore, fatigued and weak, I went out with the boys to a Lansing Lugnuts game. Perhaps there would have nothing better for my psyche that night than self-medicating immoderately in a vain attempt to exorcise my pain and forget my plight if only momentarily, but of course not. I couldn't. I was a candidate for office and God knows what a night on the town would cost me politically. Anyhow there I was, in a van filled with a bunch of old guys driving down to Lansing. Yeah, you got the picture, a bunch of guys in their 40's and 50's going to a bachelor party in the midst of my campaign. Although I knew I couldn't be a meaningful participant because I was a frickin' candidate for office, to be honest I didn't really care

DON'T VOTE FOR ME

to go out and carouse, because at 52 it was ridiculous to even be going to a bachelor party in the first place! I figured just get married, and skip the traditions. As it turned out the only guy who agreed with me was the bachelor himself, who hardly even knew any of us from his fiancée's side of the family. He had just driven fourteen hours from the East Coast and didn't need anything besides a good night's rest, something I could really have used myself.

As we traveled down to the big city, Lansing, the future place of my presumptive employment, one of my "pals" began the inquisitive process.

"*So Kevin*", he says in a long, drawn out way, "*Just how is your campaign going? Ha-ha-ha.*" And then the others joined in. "*Yeah, how's it going, Kevin?*" They sounded like a chorus of scorched cats.

"*Hey, I don't want to talk about it.*" I insisted. "*Why not Kevin?*" came a quick and insincere response. "*Look! I don't want to even think about it!*" I implored them.

It was then they all sensed they had opened a fresh cut on me and they were on me like a pack of hyenas.

"*What's the matter Kevin?!*" another one of them dug in, like a scratch against the chalkboard. "*Look!,*" I repeated emphatically, "*I-don't-want-to-talk-about-it!*"

45

DON'T VOTE FOR ME

I would have jumped out of the van if I could have. It's not that I hadn't been in similar circumstances; it was that I *had* been in similar circumstances, albeit in a previous life. A bunch of guys, a night on the town, and cold beer on a long summer night with a designated driver--believe me, I knew exactly what was going on. The vultures had a fresh road kill to feast on and there was no traffic on this highway to interrupt the buffet.

They kept up their cacophony of feigned interest, questioning every aspect of my campaign, and though I consistently tried to change the subject, they carried on. Finally I admitted I had no plan, I never did, and had given up on any expectation of success. Worst of all, I told them I wanted to drop out but my wife wouldn't let me. Well, I might as well have grabbed the steering wheel and veered off a bridge. Their heckling became even more unbearable! They knew a man was doing something he didn't want to do, and he was doing it because he didn't have the *cojones* to stand up to his wife. And worst of all, damn it, they were right. More right than they could have possibly imagined!

But I wasn't about to be gang-tackled after I had already suffered so much carnage the night before. After about 15 minutes of it, I silenced them with a 15 minute barrage of my own. Yes sir, I confess before you my brothers and sisters that I did. I dropped a 15 minute bombardment of deep blue vulgarity, launching a litany of Rod Blagojevich cuss words that preceded practically every single syllable of a most malevolent rejoinder, as Howard Cosell

DON'T VOTE FOR ME

would say. At the end of it I think they got my point. I *f'n* didn't want to *f'n* talk about it, *ad f'n-itum*. Even the Swearers Club would have sought cover from my profane tirade. I am sorry to admit this coping mechanism happened, but it did. I cannot lie. But it made it easier later that night as I righteously and indignantly declined to participate in their subsequent juvenile adventures, exploring venues promoting the lack of any literary, artistic or scientific value long after the game was over.

So there I was, reclining in the back seat of a mini-van with a like-minded burned out buddy of mine at 3:00 AM in the morning, gauging the prurient interests of the pimps and the hustlers, the college boys and the perverts, the dirty old men and the drunks, together with perhaps a few Saudi terrorists, who stumbled in and out of Lansing's south-side strip joint. All of the club's patrons were oblivious to our presence watching them from our theatre seats there in the parking lot. Finally, after an eternity, the rest of the party rejoined us and we finally headed home. I gazed out the window at the crescent moon low in the dawning sky wishing I had stayed home. Maybe if I had consumed a bellyful of Badass all the nonsense would have seemed tolerable, but since that didn't happen the entire night was like undergoing surgery without being anaesthetized. So, while my contingent of fellow passengers carried on about the varying attributes of exotic adult entertainers, I found it impossible to join in the merriment. Compounding my sense of insomnia, irascibility and isolation, I rode the complete distance home in an extremely jealous state. I

DON'T VOTE FOR ME

learned that while I spent sleepless hours in the van waiting for everyone else to call it a night, our bachelor honoree had slept through entirely everything while inside the club.

There were some silver linings I suppose. At least I hadn't been photographed cavorting with a call girl like Wilbur Mills at the Tidal Basin. But best of all, I had finally had an experience that made campaigning seem like a true chance for positive personal and spiritual growth if only by contrast to the bachelor party, a party that neither I nor the groom found very -dare I say- titillating...

DON'T VOTE FOR ME

CHAPTER VII
HIP DEEP AND SINKING

In a most peculiar way the events of that week served a purpose. In fact, all of the angst helped me to jump-start the rest of my campaign. Maybe that period of time was the cathartic experience I needed. I had been double-minded and inclined to yield too often to thinking, not doing. And I began to realize that one thing was certain after the past few days -things could only get better!

In addition to that understanding, though acknowledging the impossibility of victory, it was better to submit to my wife's more honorable view after all. Quitting is worse than losing. This was the right way to think. I just didn't want to be embarrassed by the experience. So I began. The people of my district, if they cared, would see and hear someone new and something different, because they would see and hear it from a candidate who said something no other candidate had ever said before:

"Do not vote for me"

... And this is how I put it in my brochure

"I am a lawyer with a record of twenty years of public service. This qualification distinguishes me from all the others in this race. Does it make sense to complain so much about

49

DON'T VOTE FOR ME

government, yet count on it to solve all our problems? As an attorney all too often I have seen our State's policies reward irresponsibility. That must stop.

Our way of life depends on an innovative and progressive approach to the future. The people of the 93rd District need a representative who understands the law, and will provide common sense solutions for today's ever changing world.

But government cannot and should not provide all things to all people. Do not vote for me unless you are willing to help shoulder your share of the load."

Yes. That is what I wrote. *Don't vote for me.* In an eerie way it protected my psyche from assured defeat. I hoped some voters might understand my deeper meaning and if so perhaps I could escape a last place finish. But there wasn't much time left.

I had considered going door to door but I was dissuaded by the fact that for every positive result invariably there would be four negative, ten unanswered doors, and twenty non-committals. Even if I had the temperament to withstand failure 34 times out of 35, I did not have the time to do it. It wasn't possible as I worked full time in a real job throughout the campaign.

Ultimately I decided that my best chance to make a difference was to perform well in the three scheduled debates and hope to garner the type of local media coverage one might expect.

DON'T VOTE FOR ME

That was really the only way I could present my views and credentials. The debates were scheduled for St. Johns, Ithaca and Alma, the three largest municipalities in the district. In addition, with my wife's assistance, I wrote to each township board requesting the opportunity to speak before them, and although only a few responded, I gladly accepted their invitations.

I was scheduled to make a presentation to both the Clinton and Gratiot County Republican Committees, and also reluctantly agreed to participate in every local parade through the primary. I answered every questionnaire submitted to me by the local news publications. I always found the time to give talks or presentations to local clubs or civic groups as opportunities arose. Looking back I am relatively astonished at how much I did do in so little time, but more often than not I felt I was doing nothing more than treading water.

Finally, I had to get out some kind of literature to the voter. To do that, my wife obtained voter registration logs. A computer savvy supporter put together an excellent website for me, which presented in my own words all that I wanted to convey to the voters. My neighbor literally wore her fingers to the bone, addressing envelopes by hand for days on end. She was doing something for me I could never have asked her to do. I know I wouldn't have done it myself. Day after day I picked up boxes of hand-addressed envelopes from her to mail, knowing darn well 99% of it would end up in someone's garbage without a second thought.

DON'T VOTE FOR ME

But efforts like hers and that of others in my campaign kept me from giving up before the race was done. I became a real candidate, preparing to walk in my first parade in Ashley, Michigan. I had magnetic campaign signs on each side of my car, a 2002 bright yellow Pontiac Aztek. To decorate my *"float,"* I duct-taped an American flag to the hatch back window. *Yeah! That would get their attention!* I often amused myself by thinking like that. *Why not?*

It was a beautiful day and all of the floats and paraders congregated on a side street of a depressed downtown business community that somehow held together in spite of the realities of Michigan's economy. There were a lot of people gathering to watch the parade. The numbers for such a small town surprised me. As my son drove the Aztek through the parade route in Ashley, I followed behind on foot handing out my campaign brochures. It was my first genuine day of personal contact with the public of the district, and it all went much too quickly. I was the only person handing out my literature, and soon I was forced to run most of the route, for it was impossible to keep up with the pace of the car. People were lined up on both sides of the street. Running back and forth across the street I had no time to talk to people. Soon my Aztek was blocks ahead of me, pushed ahead by the other vehicles behind it along the parade route. As I handed out my brochures, although almost everyone was friendly, it was entirely obvious to me that most did not constitute the type of person that would be expected to vote in a primary. I was right; my

DON'T VOTE FOR ME

cost/benefit analysis of it was 99% cost, 1% benefit. And that, I thought, was a positive assessment!

I met only one person who showed any interest at all, but that was offset by another person who was entirely antagonistic. That one negative encounter bothered me and made me somewhat angry, because I was deriving little pleasure in being hot, sweaty, out of breath, and acting as a Republican pin-cushion for voters who had a problem that summer with George Bush. I was not doing this for fun, not that the spectators cared. They think politicians enjoy their little parades! Here is a little secret, people: *Trust me*, candidates hate them!

Well, at least I finally got to meet all five of my Republican primary opponents at one event. I went up to each of them to introduce myself beforehand. All, with the exception of Greg Carlson, brought plenty of support with them. Their scores of volunteers handed out trinkets, candy, cards, and literature to the observers. Anyhow, the lesson I learned was nothing more than what I already knew. I was a serious underdog, and not only to Opsommer. All of the others not only had a plan, they were well into the process of its execution.

From here on, we started to see a lot of each other. All of the candidates were invited to the "Michigan Livestock Farmers Board of *Influence Peddlers*." That was not their official name, but I'll call them that. The purpose of our meeting with them was to reverently bow down and try to gain their endorsement in the

DON'T VOTE FOR ME

primary. Though I felt like a hypocrite at the cemetery, I suffered no pangs of guilt for attending this examination. If they wanted a pro-agriculture voice from this group, I was their man. Unhappily, it didn't turn out that way. In fact, I nearly got clobbered by a farm gal who gave me the most blood curdling stare and reprisal of my campaign!

The meeting took place in Ithaca. All of the candidates checked in and waited in line as if preparing for an examination of one's conscience in the confessional. Everything was way behind schedule, which I found extremely aggravating, as I had to stand around and make small talk with several other candidates waiting their turn.

While we were waiting, Josh Nunez told me that he was campaigning door to door 12 to 14 hours a day, and from time to time his young children campaigned by his side. I didn't envy him, but I felt extremely sorry for his kids. I asked, *"Do they like doing that?"* He assured me that they loved it. Jokingly, I said, *"It sounds like child abuse to me."* For the record, in fact, they did love their daddy. He was a good father and a good man and they enjoyed politicking.

Josh was an interesting guy. He was a good speaker, and was certainly an arch-conservative. He informed his audiences that he had a money back guarantee. If elected, he promised to return 100% of his campaign contributions to his financial supporters should he ever violate his promise never to vote for a

DON'T VOTE FOR ME

tax increase. He railed against government waste, and indeed governmental spending in general. So it was somewhat curious to find while I was doing a door to door literature drop of my own, that someone from the Nunez campaign had distributed hundreds of unsolicited taxpayer supported official State of Michigan Department of Transportation maps, rubber-banded to his campaign literature, throughout several precincts in Alma and St. Louis. Counter intuitive? Governmental waste? I'm not saying it wasn't a good idea, I'm just saying... I report... you decide.

Anyhow, I felt like just blowing the whole thing off, but after speaking with the others who had to endure the same long delay, I capitulated to the thought that I had to do things like this or else none of these farmers would know about my support of agriculture in America.

As it turned out, I would have been right to go my own way. I was less than impressed by this panel of modern day farmers and they were far less impressed with me. In my fantasy world, farmers were supposed to be the underdogs. I remembered a time when they mostly were small, independent, and somewhat self-sufficient, and as long as government stayed out of their lives they got by. You know... the *'don't tread on me'* types. Farmers still act that way, just so no one ever takes advantage of him or her. They always play the simple old country boy. But more often than not these days, they are light years smarter than the general public, especially in their dealings with government programs. Nevertheless, I am very pro-farmer, even in regards to modern day

DON'T VOTE FOR ME

mega-farmers, provided they don't play mind games with me. You would think some of them still milk cows by hand, and break the land with a team of oxen.

The inquisition began. I was asked my opinion of the biggest problem facing agriculture. I replied that it wasn't the disappearance of the small and marginally competent farmer, but rather it is the ever-present temptation of any farmer who is not capable of running a business based on economies of scale, to *"cash out"* and sell good agricultural land to developers. Well, a few of them nodded weakly to that answer. I should have realized that these people couldn't care less about *"hobby farmers"* in that situation; they were all about themselves and *"their"* circumstances. They weren't concerned at all about the old 90-acre farm. No, they were talking about Concentrated Animal Feeding Operations (CAFO's), environmental regulations, and about right to farm legislation that would allow them to do things to the environment for which other companies, manufacturers and individuals could and would be severely fined, punished, or put out of business. And they were sure to bring up their concerns in that regard. So they asked me about the modern trend of agriculture, to which the board seemed to be entirely oriented.

"Well," I said, *"large scale farming is a reality, and our society must adjust to it. But I don't have much use for these ultra huge farms, with the mass manufacturing of beef and milk with feed lots and all the manure lagoons around the nation stinking up the countryside."*

DON'T VOTE FOR ME

Well, I stepped into a 640-acre cow pie when I said that! The woman heretofore mentioned on the panel stared daggers at me.

Through grinding teeth, she pronounced, *"I own a dairy farm like that, and I don't appreciate your remarks!"*

"Well," I countered, *"maybe a lot of us think farmers who operate as corporate agri-businesses should find a better way of dealing with waste. I am not saying you can't have a large operation, but maybe you should look into methane energy production, or do something productive with all of it."*

"Well, for your information, we do!" she exclaimed, clenching her fists.

"Oh, you do?" I replied, unconvinced.

"Yes, as a matter of fact!" she shouted. "We use **all** of it for fertilizer!!!"

I thought she was going to come across the table at me! I hit the dirt like I was getting out of the way of a high and tight Justin Verlander fastball. Fortunately she was not armed with a pitchfork! I would have liked to question the accuracy of that answer, but I didn't dare. Perhaps in her case it was true, but for some in the mega-industrial corporate agricultural community at large, I am quite certain such claims are just more BS. Some

DON'T VOTE FOR ME

farmers may use their voluminous waste for fertilizer on their land, but some of the extreme amounts of urine and fecal matter often end up elsewhere, and like herbicides and pesticides in the mega-farming industry -the excess runs downhill and downstream.

I never intended to pick on farmers. I realize farming is a difficult and vital enterprise, and I understand the need for statutory deference, yet I was branded an enemy to agriculture and my interview only got worse after that. So, speaking of waste, it was another wasted night. I wasn't counting on their PAC money. From the start I refused to solicit or accept special interest money, but now I could forget about their support at the polls. I found throughout the campaign that it was a complete waste of time to be honest with any special interest group. That is not seen as virtuous to them. It's all about ingratiating yourself to them.

After I got thrown out of the turnip truck on Ithaca's back roads, I got up and dusted myself off. I can be a country boy, too - hard-headed and stubborn when I put my mind to the task. I didn't care if I got their support. I was going to speak my mind if nothing else. By this time if I was in for a penny, I was in for a pound.

What I didn't realize until late in the campaign was how many uses manure may serve not only in agri-business, but in local politics as well. So, hold on, the subject will surface again. Candidate Tim Black made sure of that. Boy, oh boy ...*did he ever!*

DON'T VOTE FOR ME

CHAPTER VIII
SIGNS OF THINGS TO COME

Right around that same time period, I met with the respective executive officers of both the Clinton and Gratiot County Republican Party. The Clinton County committee seemed interested in the veracity of my Republican credentials, as I was not a Party regular by their standards. I had never even been a precinct delegate. Although it was a well attended function everyone who attended the Clinton affair had already either tacitly or openly supported an opponent of mine. I had no entrenched Party support at all. Though I felt they gave me a fair welcome, it was a perfunctory exercise at best. Gratiot County was the wild west of the district as five of the six candidates were Clinton County residents, but even so most candidates had already carved out wide swaths of support there as well. Paul Opsommer was the darling of the business community. Josh Nunez seemed to have garnered the fundamentalist sector. Mike Trebesh had good support in the agricultural sector, but also had liaisons in Alma due to his prior relationship with Alma College as a professor in accounting. Greg Carlson was a Gratiot County Commissioner and had more local contacts than any of us. Finally there was Tim Black who did continuous and extensive door-to-door campaigning and reportedly hired a professional Lansing-based polling firm to assist him in targeting voters.

Opsommer, Trebesh and I were invited to speak with the

DON'T VOTE FOR ME

Gratiot County Republicans. It was held the very evening RTL formally endorsed the Opsommer campaign. That night was the first time I empathized with Mike Trebesh; RTL's effect was palpable. As for Paul, I didn't begrudge him, but I felt he didn't deserve their endorsement any more than any of the rest of us. All five of his opponents felt like Michigan RTL lied to us, and Paul took full advantage of it. I let Gratiot County know some very curious things were happening behind the scenes in that regard and that I hoped they would keep an open mind.

Their chairman was a lawyer. I was very impressed by his command, intelligence, fairness and objectivity. He told us that Gratiot County was in the process of putting together a debate with the promise of substantial voter attendance and press coverage too. My hopes soared hearing he anticipated a crowd of 300 nonaligned primary voters! So far I had met very few people who seemed to care about the campaign in Clinton County, and our one and only debate there had already come and gone. In the Clinton County debate about 100 people attended, if that. Not one member of the local press covered that event in St. Johns. Notably absent was the Lansing State Journal whose editorial board presumably would and later did, endorse Paul Opsommer. Big surprise. Even more incredible was the absence of the *Clinton County News* at that debate.

Nevertheless, the issues of the campaign focused on abortion (as always), the Michigan single business tax, home schooling, affirmative action and bipartisanship. Oh yeah, gay

DON'T VOTE FOR ME

marriage too. What I wanted to talk about was finding ways to make genuine progress on energy production, and more specifically on local domestic energy production. Let's face it: Americans are not going to consume less energy in the future, no matter what conservation measures are taken. Somehow politicians always manage to evade giving us real solutions. I think perhaps it is because the press just doesn't pound on the issue.

I was rather amused, if not honored, to find that the Michigan Human Rights Council gave me a score of *"somewhat negative"* on issues concerning racial, economic, sexual orientation, illegal immigration, and abortion rights. I was amused because every other Republican in my primary race had scored an *"unacceptable"* rating. I can only assume that I got a D+ on their report card because I recognize reality when it comes to legislating behavior. I don't believe in affirmative action based on race, but I'm okay with affirmative action based on income. It shouldn't take a genius to figure out that Barry Bond's kids do not deserve a leg up in education or employment assistance over poor pale-faced children from a trailer park. Neither should it take a genius to conclude that since blacks clearly suffer disproportionate economic disadvantages, the effect of switching to economic-based affirmative action would continue to proportionally aid blacks more so than other segments of our population. I would support an affirmative action program amended in this non-raced based fashion. This simple change would recognize the progress we have made, yet acknowledge we have a long way to go. End

DON'T VOTE FOR ME

result: a win-win for everyone.

I supported the traditional definition of marriage, but I didn't oppose the concept of civil unions. I didn't think gay couples should be on par with heterosexual couples seeking to adopt because I think more study and research is required before society advances such a law. Until then, advancing such a proposition can only be based on an article of faith, or an anecdotal event; human history is not replete with stories of success in that regard. True, there are few examples of failure either, but we just don't know. To me, as a progressive conservative, I place the burden of proof on the group advocating change. When it involves the upbringing of someone else's child, that burden is extraordinary in my judgment.

I didn't believe in rounding up undocumented non-citizen residents, but after allowing a reasonable grace period for mandatory compliance, I had no problem with swift and secure deportation for those who continue to refuse to comply with our laws. Everyone knows it is a problem that will not been solved by PC/BS. It has to stop.

Finally, although I didn't know much about stem-cell research, it seemed to make sense to the scientific community and to the medical profession. Unhappily the whole question had become political. We live in a new paradigm of competing life and death issues. In short, ethically we seem to have outrun our coverage. If we are ever going to achieve the enlightenment to

DON'T VOTE FOR ME

understand nature's permissible boundaries, I don't know how the politics of today can get us there. In my debates I referenced a great article written by Peggy Noonan, who at the time expressed her frustration -and mine- that the issue is quite possibly an irresolvable political dilemma.

Though the debates would prove to be my favorite campaign memories, they were a small part of the process. I learned that putting up and preparing signs was the singular and extraordinarily time consuming part of campaigning. I easily put a few thousand miles on my Aztek driving from one end of the district to the other putting up 4' x 4' yard signs. Putting signs up dominated my life for weeks on end. First my wife ordered 200 yard signs. With my wife, family, friends and co-workers working together, the signs were dispensed fairly quickly, but to put them in the ground was another story. It looked simple, but soon everyone became exasperated by the annoying task of forcing the galvanized aluminum shafts of the framing into the corrugated plastic openings of the sign itself! Some signs came together like hand in glove, but others were impossible, like trying to force a square peg into a round hole. There was no rhyme or reason to success. Sometimes we could put together 10 straight signs without a hitch, but then the next 10 would take 30 minutes of our time. Then there was the question of quality of the ground. Some lawns were soft and the signs practically sunk into the earth. Other lawns were hard as concrete and the wire supports twisted, bent and failed. Once the galvanized wire frame failed, you were left with a

DON'T VOTE FOR ME

worthless, sorry, and limp waste of three dollars and more wasted time. It happened a lot. But even if everything went well, a stiff wind might also leave a sign poorly displayed. Then you had the thieves and pranksters. At least they were equal opportunity ne'er do wells. Although everyone in the primary lost signs that way, the expenses caught up with me in a hurry. Nevertheless, I was able to distribute two hundred signs throughout Clinton County, but I had not yet scratched the surface in Gratiot County. My wife ordered 200 more in the hopes I could find places for them there, but whether that would happen depended on the success of my debate there. Anyhow, that was the plan.

After exhausting our supply of the small yard signs, my father-in-law and my sons began the process of driving in the more durable 4x4 stenciled signs. They looked sharp: black lettering outlined in yellow with a white background, left my name highly visible. Though it took a lot of effort to cut and paint each sign by hand, more difficult was finding the right locations where signs were visible to lots of motorists. One of the most ridiculous aspects of this whole process of sign-making was the need to comply with election law. Each sign had to include the printed disclaimer:

"*Paid for by the Committee to Elect Kevin Hayes.*"

Now this was entirely stupid not only because there was no real *"Committee,"* but even dumber was that the disclaimer on each sign was hand written by me in tiny lettering made with a

DON'T VOTE FOR ME

Sharpie, as if it could actually be seen by anyone, much less from the highway at a speed of 70 mph. But who knows? Maybe someone might pull over and take a roll in the weeds like I did. I'm sure they would be happy to see that I had complied with the law. What nonsense.

Putting up large signs took far more effort than I thought it would. First, you had to drive in wooden stakes. Then screw the ½ inch particleboard into the stakes, one in the back of the sign and then the other on the opposite side, kitty corner in front to provide stability. It worked well, except for a few occasions, which of course always seemed to occur at my best sites. One of them involved simply putting a sign at the professional offices located at State Road and Business 27 in Dewitt Township. An attorney friend of mine told me to put a *"big one"* up at that location. When I got there with my son, I tried to telephone him to determine exactly where he wanted us to put it because it was a much larger office complex than I expected. However, I was unable to reach him. Not wanting to turn back and make this another wasted trip, I made my best guess as to a proper location. The stakes went in easily and within a minute or two I had a primo site for a 4x4 sign. It was a coup! Thousands of Clinton County residents passed that particular location daily! Best of all it was up before the upcoming 4th of July holiday. I convinced myself that things were improving.

That weekend, I left for St. Ignace finally feeling pretty good about the campaign. We were invited to a wedding, and

DON'T VOTE FOR ME

unlike the bachelor party from the previous month, I was having a wonderful respite from the campaign. That is, until I made the mistake of logging on to my campaign website at the hotel and checking email. A major Lansing area business office leasing company accused me of destroying its entire sprinkler system on the property where my son and I had just put up that sign before we left for the wedding.

Damn it all! I could only imagine what that would cost: $5,000? $10,000? $50,000? I had no idea. I talked it over with my son, *"When you drove in the stakes, did you hit something hard... like a pipe?"* I asked.

"No," he assured me.

"Neither did I, but some guy is saying we ruined their sprinkler system!"

Neither one of us saw any water or leaks or anything that indicated damage, but how could we prove otherwise? I knew that nobody was going to feel sorry for a politician! If I had to go to court over his alleged damages, I'd better have a good defense. I had my 17-year-old son, and my word, but the real evidence was a foot or two underground, and I was 250 miles away. The truth was that I didn't know the truth. Maybe we broke a pipeline, but it sure didn't seem like we did. So I called the agent on my cell phone right away. He wasn't in. For half a day, on what was to be a nice sabbatical, I was floundering in a sea of political malaise. I

DON'T VOTE FOR ME

thought to myself, *"how can anyone but millionaire candidates put up with all this angst?"* There was no pay off in this gambit. There was no rainbow, much less a pot of gold. So there I was, a lawyer, an assistant prosecuting attorney, being pummeled once again against the ropes by the threat of treble damages from a big-time property developer. *"Don't quit,"* I muttered under my breath. Right. How could I get off a roller coaster ride from hell half way upside down?

A lot of worrying dampened my day before I finally received a return call. I decided beforehand to be kind, apologetic and nice to the agent. So I told him that I didn't intend any harm, that I thought I had permission, and that my son and I did not think we had hit anything or done any damage. But I'll pay for whatever I damaged. It was the right thing to do.

And then a miracle came my way. *"Well,"* he said. *"That's okay. It really didn't do much damage. In fact it didn't break the pipe. It just brushed its side. Everything is okay. We just can't have your sign there."*

I let out a huge sigh of relief. I felt like he was just messing with me all along, but I welcomed the news. *"Uh, can I get my sign back?"* I sheepishly asked. Well, of course he didn't have it anymore. So another $10 or so down the drain. Another two hours or so going there and putting it up wasted. Another prime spot lost at the most prime of times. But I had to feel good. I saved $50,000... at least that's how a politician would spin it. So I

67

DON'T VOTE FOR ME

dodged another bullet. I survived another hellish descent. After the brief wedding recess we crossed the Mackinac Bridge and headed home for the next uphill climb. The 4th of July parade in Westphalia was the next adventure on my agenda.

After the long weekend, I couldn't convince anyone to join me. So there I was, all alone in my yellow Aztek. Nothing like your posse having your back. I had 500 brochures with me, but no driver, and no help. This of course was pathetic, but by this time I was used to it. I was beginning to wonder if perhaps I should vote for one of the other guys myself. But how could I blame others for not coming with me to these insipid summer traditions? I wouldn't either, if the shoe was on the other foot. One parade a summer is more than enough, yet I had several more to go. As far as I was concerned you were damned if you did, and damned if you didn't. Voters couldn't care less if you were there, but they'd be sure to hold it against you if you weren't. So there you go. It's the American way.

I was trying to figure out just how I was going to participate in this parade. How could I both drive and hand out brochures? Miraculously, an Opsommer supporter actually recruited a driver for me! I offered the young man $10, but he agreed to drive my Aztek for free. I'm sure he felt sorry for me. Anyhow, that was mighty kind of him, and it fired me up to work the crowd. Once again outnumbered by my opponents' workers 100:1, I hustled the route handing out as many of my campaign pieces as I could. Again for the second straight parade, I couldn't

DON'T VOTE FOR ME

shake one hand. I was too busy handing out all my brochures, running and trying to stay within a mile of my car.

Still, it was a beautiful day and the parade had its moments. Westphalia is about 110% German Catholic, and along the route I met an elderly Catholic nun. As I was about to hand her a brochure she informed me she wasn't a Michigan voter -she was from Chicago and in town just visiting her relatives. I suggested, *"From what I hear of Chicago politics, I don't think that should preclude you from voting anywhere, anytime, dead or alive."* She laughed so heartily at my suggestion that she probably had to go to confession afterwards. For me it was a bonus because her relatives got a great chuckle out of that remark as well.

Later, I ran into a shirt-tail relative of my wife's who noticed my brochure's reference to my 17 year marriage. He jokingly asked if that was a qualification for office -to which I replied, *"I can't say it is for everyone, but in my case it most definitely is."* He burst out laughing. These two encounters were nice. A candidate always appreciates his wit being acknowledged. It made my day.

Finally I met my first heckler. He was a teenager maybe 15 or 16 years old. I don't remember what he was saying but it was something vulgar and rude. I am sure he didn't expect me to run right over to him and throw my arm over his shoulder and ask him if he was old enough to vote, so of course that is exactly what I did. When he told me he wasn't, I told him, *"So now that I know*

DON'T VOTE FOR ME

you aren't 18, I don't have to kiss your butt. I guess I can just go ahead and insult you too!" We both laughed. It was all in good fun.

I suppose I had a pretty good time for being so alone. But it didn't pay to be there. The final tally would show I got four votes from Westphalia -maybe two from the nun, and one each from the kid and my distant relative.

Afterwards, it was back to the old grind. I went back down to Lansing to replace the sign at the site of the sprinkler fiasco. After I replaced it, within a week that sign disappeared. This time I gave up. The primo site was not so primo after all. Other signs were misappropriated from splendid locations throughout the county. The tragedy was that almost all of these efforts took genius to place the signs as I did. I could have made a big deal about it with the police but I was beyond such trifles. All I wanted were my signs back, but they were never returned.

My *piece de la resistance* was the 4x4 sign on property located at the cloverleaf of I-69 and US 127. It required that I lift the sign about four feet off the ground in order to make it visible above the limited access fencing separating the highway from a residential backyard. This property was about 25 miles from my house but when I got there I discovered I did not bring sufficient framing wood to provide for an elevated platform. I had to make it happen. I checked around the owner's property for some scrap wood. Finally, I located a few pieces behind his garage. They

DON'T VOTE FOR ME

appeared to be in good shape, even though they had probably been there since the highway was built several years before. I *"borrowed"* a few of those scraps, but still had to find a stronger backing for the 4x4 sign itself, as its four foot elevation was certain to require the added strength to deal with prevailing western winds.

Luckily I saw some abandoned pallets right over the side of the fence on highway property. So, I hopped over and scored one of them. I drilled screws through the sign into the pallet. Then I screwed the stakes in between the slats on the pallet. Finally I was able to elevate the sign, and tack the stakes to scrap wood, which provided posts for the sign. It worked beautifully, saving me several hours of time at a minimum. Small miracles like that gave me inordinate pleasure and pride. Ah, if the voters could have seen me work out of such difficulties! They would know I could easily manage any political crisis!

That was my last large sign. I wanted more, but did not care to make any new purchases of OSB board. By now every dime I spent was coming out of my family budget. As luck would have it, I ran into a farmer who I had supported in an earlier election for the office of drain commissioner. He told me he had a bunch of old campaign signs, which I was welcome to use. When I learned they were also 4x4 signs, I gladly accepted, knowing of course I would have to paint over them. So off I went to his barn near Francis Road and made a daring climb up to the loft of his storage barn. The ladder to the loft was extremely narrow, technical, and quite dangerous. Though I was in fairly good shape,

DON'T VOTE FOR ME

and believed I could have negotiated the rickety ladder and carry down one cumbersome sign at a time, it would have taken me at least a day or two, assuming I would survive each descent. After trying to do it twice, I decided it was simply far too life-threatening. I was going to stop altogether, or go to plan B. But, *there was no plan B*. His wife was at the barn with me, and I expressed to her my difficulty. *"Boy, I need to find an easier way. Is there any other way to access the loft?"*

"Well," she said, *"there is a door that swings out back of the barn, but you would have to be careful -there are lots of gaps in the flooring and it is a long way down."*

I would take my chances. I swung the second story gate open facing the yard far below. It was probably a good 15-20 feet to the ground, and there was no way to hand down the 4x4 boards. There was only one solution: *air resistance.* One by one, I brought the signs to the big opening and softly flung the signs like a Frisbee in the direction of my trusty Aztek. It was truly a risky operation, but once again a little creativity and efficiency led to a lucky result. My Aztek's back end was the perfect size to allow me to stack about 20 or 30 signs. The best thing about that experience was the view of the countryside from the backside of the barn. *Wow!* It was the classic bucolic scene of the land of plenty –green and golden fields promising a coming abundant harvest. I could have stood on that beam for an hour just watching the wind create a living work of art before my eyes, but no, I had to go home right away and paint over the old lettering and redo

DON'T VOTE FOR ME

them with my own stenciling. It was another violation of a Sunday day of rest. I had no choice. I had a full week of my day job ahead of me.

When I got home, I took out the sawhorses and the sticky oil based paint and set everything up on the driveway. It was a hot and windy day -perfect drying weather I thought. I was about half finished with the job when gnarly looking storm clouds started to form above me. The fate of another entire day's work hung in the balance. Absolutely everything I had just painted was outside. A hard rain would ruin everything. Anyhow, I decided to keep on painting and trust in God. Yes, you can be sure I prayed. I prayed a lot. I prayed just for survival, for sanity, for another day to pass, for liberation from my self-imposed political prison. What was I doing? I didn't know. All I knew was that whatever I was doing at the time I wanted it to get done and not have to re-do it. That really was all there was to it. There was not time to be philosophic about it. Anyhow, my prayers worked. It didn't rain.

There were several significant events remaining: parades in Alma, Elsie and Fowler, the big Ithaca debate, and the final debate at Alma College. The campaign was quickly winding down, but I was still scrambling to do the things which I should have done well before I filed for office. Now I realized that Mike Trebesh knew exactly what he was doing a year earlier. I was expending a tremendous amount of physical and mental energy doing simple and not so simple tasks that had nothing to do with securing votes. It was all too often manual labor and field

DON'T VOTE FOR ME

engineering, not public relations.

As I drove home, I was resigned to accept that this whole process required a lot more help from the outside world. I needed to get my message out. I needed extensive press coverage. I needed a *cause célèbre*. And the promised remedy was the Ithaca debate coming up the next week.

All I wanted now was a chance to really be heard. I just wanted a chance to sound off, to speak my mind, to be understood, and not get cut off in the process. Unfortunately, that did not happen. In fact, it could not have been worse.

DON'T VOTE FOR ME

CHAPTER IX

I AM A RACIST

I never felt better about my campaign than I did after the Gratiot County debate in Ithaca. Few of my answers were rehearsed, and I had no nervousness whatsoever. Unfortunately, there were nowhere near the 300 people their Republican chairman predicted. Sadly, once again there were about 100 in attendance at best, and two-thirds of them were obviously directly involved in someone's campaign. I had 10 people there on my behalf. I was happy they came, because I think they saw for themselves I could easily hold my own against the others.

My focus in the debate centered on youth. No one in the primary had yet addressed their futures or their needs. Michigan's youth were totally ignored. I said I wanted to see Mid-Michigan transformed into a Mecca of energy production, that I was sick and tired of the lies and propaganda of the Washington-based energy lobbyists who continually claimed they were unable to construct an oil refinery in America. That was curious, I suggested, because the oil industry had no problem tearing down the only refinery in my district. It was located in Alma, whose citizens, workers, and city officials begged the company to keep it in operation.

I argued that Michigan the perfect and natural location for nuclear production. We have splendid universities, abundant fresh water, and an industrial manufacturing base in need of power. In

DON'T VOTE FOR ME

fact, we could be exporters of power throughout the Midwest. It was rumored that Alma was considering constructing a coal-fired plant, with CO2 trapping technology. All well and good, I said, but we should incorporate nuclear power into a national energy solution. I said it was time to correct our nation's response to the Three Mile Island incident from 1977. In spite of the recent extraordinary misfortunes at Fukushima, I remain a proponent of nuclear energy. Although problems remain, it is clear that technology today is far more sophisticated than it was at the time those plants were constructed.

Concerning our mammoth trade imbalance due to our imports of foreign oil, I said Republican John Anderson had the right idea way back in 1980 when he proposed a nation-wide 50 cent per gallon tax on gasoline, a penalty of sorts, but a proposal that would help hasten the day when our nation would be free of its oil dependency.

"But," I acknowledged, *"that proposal cost him any chance of the Republican presidential nomination and I am not about to commit the same mistake. So don't think I'm suggesting that for Michigan."* The room erupted with laughter. In any event, Anderson was proved right. We are more dependent than ever.

On the Affirmative Action ballot proposal, I left voters no doubt that I detested race-based governmental programs. *"If we are such a racist nation,"* I argued, *"then why are people from*

DON'T VOTE FOR ME

Africa, Jamaica, Haiti and elsewhere breaking down our doors to immigrate here? And besides, why should their children be equated with American descendants of slaves merely by virtue of their African ancestry? And beyond that, why should the incredibly wealthy and advantaged such as Barry Bond's children receive any benefits under an affirmative action program?"

I have to admit it was easy pickings to rail against old Barry that summer.

I carried on. *"I do believe, however, in affirmation action based on income and merit. Those less fortunate should be considered for available governmental assistance provided they otherwise qualify. In reality this system will disproportionately favor African-Americans because they are statistically and disproportionately disadvantaged."* Then I went on to say, *"I don't believe in quotas. But if I was a white cop in Detroit, you better believe I would want a black cop for my partner."* That's exactly what I said and I meant it. Some people may call that quota thinking. I call it common sense.

The debate moderator asked me what was the biggest problem in the State of Michigan and what would I do to solve it. I answered it by saying, *"It is the Detroit Lions, and my solution is to coax Barry Sanders out of retirement."* Then I returned to the real theme of my campaign: the future of Michigan's youth.

No one in the primary could possibly have had the amount

DON'T VOTE FOR ME

of contact I had had with our District's young people. For the previous decade and a half, I saw thousands of young people in the pre-trials our office conducts in District Court every Friday. They came in for a variety of reasons, but usually their indiscretions involve underage drinking, possession of marijuana, or a driving infraction. None of these misdemeanors are grave, unforgivable sins. Truth be told, we all know many more people have committed these types of offenses than have ever been caught, that's for sure. Most of them seem like decent, but directionless kids, yet nothing bothered me more than to hear so many of them tell me on far too many occasions of the economic plight they brought upon themselves due to having or fathering babies out of wedlock.

Our court system is flooded with the social problems brought on by generations of babies having babies having babies. Well, babies are not really having babies -the truth is irresponsible unwed birth parents are doing so, who are neither ashamed of such irresponsibility nor care to develop the discipline or acquire the means to give their child joint parenting in a traditional familial setting. These youth have presumably been aware of the facts of life well in advance of metamorphosing into our society's sexualized youth. They have been afforded every form of contraceptive. These youth have been told, taught, warned, threatened, and cajoled into becoming responsible sexual persons. And still they fail a parent's first serious obligation: their duty concerning reproduction. To reproduce without commitment is

DON'T VOTE FOR ME

like eating without working. There is no law against it, but it is a sin nevertheless, a great sin in my mind, more so than most crimes.

Therefore, our courts have had to step in and become super-parents, using scarce funds to place infants with too many similarly neglected half brothers, step-sisters, cousins, friends and neighbors who are being brought up more often than not by child protective services, foster parents, or by old and tired grandparents if they are lucky, while the rest of society is taxed to the extreme. The public cannot imagine the inordinate amounts of money taxpayers waste on these *"parents"* teaching them after the fact how to put the horse before the cart. Unfortunately, by the time court ordered services are in play, the horse is already out of the barn. This problem has long been epidemic in America's African-American community and more and more it was becoming an acceptable social practice in all segments of our society.

I asked myself, how did this happen? And why did our government look the other way for so many years, paying lip service to family values, supposedly looking out for our children? There is no doubt whatsoever that a mess has been created by our social acceptance of out of wedlock births and the attendant ills that too often accompany the phenomenon. The cycle of poverty, illiteracy, dependency, ignorance, prejudice, crime and underemployment are all fruits of this alarmingly absurd, irresponsible and carcinogenic national time-bomb.

So I dared to suggest the unthinkable: In order to conceive

DON'T VOTE FOR ME

a child, parents should first be licensed, and that license would be called a marriage license, which was common thinking when I was a child, but revolutionary today, I admit. Anyhow, I continued carrying on, *"Young urban girls should not be having babies…"* and at *that* exact moment the moderator cut me off mid-sentence.

I wasn't allowed to complete my point, as I was timed out. I intended to continue and say that the prevalence of out-of wedlock births was no longer just happening in cities like Lansing, but was now common place and acceptable in every circumstance in urban, suburban and rural America -yes even here in the 93rd District -and it is a problem that needs to be tackled. I requested the opportunity to complete my point, but the moderator adamantly refused. At the break I approached the reporters covering the debate to clarify the remark, but they did not take any notice of it, so I let it go and thought nothing more of it.

The debate concluded and I felt totally upbeat for running. I felt I had proved myself and I think the audience and my opponents thought so too. Several people came up to me afterward and asked for a sign, telling me that I was the one candidate who had come across as genuine and realistic. A reporter covering the debate just looked at me and asked, *"Just who are you?"* It was already July 18 and the political reporter for Gratiot County's largest paper had just learned of my existence. I told her about my last minute decision to run, my lack of financing, and my trial and error strategy of campaigning, with emphasis on error. Thereafter, she proved to be the one and only reporter who actually covered

DON'T VOTE FOR ME

the campaign, and covered it fairly.

I knew I had saved face in Ithaca, and that I could hold my own against the others in front of any crowd, and now I finally believed I was going to get at least 53 votes! It was the first time I went to bed happy and satisfied with my decision to run for office. I was happy with everything.

But the very next morning my life became a living nightmare.

In little less than 12 hours my psyche turned a complete 180. I don't know what it is like to be an African-American and suffer the indignity of a racial slur, but I know it must be bad all around. However I now know what it is like to be painted as a racist and I can tell you how that feels. Believe me I know, and here is how it happened. When I returned to work after the Ithaca debate a co-worker approached me in a very excitable attitude. A report was going around the entire courthouse that in the Ithaca debate I said that *"black girls shouldn't be having babies."* He told me that one of our judges was highly dubious about the report, but curious if in fact I had actually made such a declaration. Although the allegation was preposterous, it was a sucker-punch the likes of which I'd never experienced. After I composed myself, I was soon able to verify I was indeed being painted as a bigot and a racist from an undeterminable source. Well, I am not one to turn the other cheek. I knew exactly what I had said the night before in Ithaca, how and what happened and where I stood.

DON'T VOTE FOR ME

I readily admitted to an incomplete dissertation on my part about the subject concerning out of wedlock births because I had been cut off, but even then what I had said was absolutely without racial connotation, code or animus. But what really ticked me off was that somebody did not have the courage or the dignity to confront me about my remarks before impugning my name among my co-workers-people who had known me for seventeen years, and in many cases longer. My position was not a secret: For weeks it had been posted on my election website for all to see. In my effort to bring local attention to a problem that cuts across all segments of our society, I was immolated by the fiery charge of racism.

I was so livid that I called the judge and left a very terse message. I was outraged, but I knew it wasn't her fault. In my message I referenced my website for accuracy. My call was promptly returned and after I explained everything, the courthouse firestorm was quickly put out. Even so, when all was said and done, the vestiges of rumor and innuendo always smolder. As far as I was concerned the air remained filled with the smoke and stench of arson.

I had no idea who started the rumor and who was so quick to slander me, but I hoped to find out in a big way. This was a personal attack; far different in degree or scope than anything I had suffered in the campaign. Everything else was minute by comparison. An allegation like that could lead to disbarment from the practice of law and the termination of my employment, not to

DON'T VOTE FOR ME

mention the effect it would have upon my family. I can't and don't want to remember if I had ever felt angrier in my life. But I can assure you a day was coming when I would. *Quickly.*

In any event, I felt that I had acquitted myself of the charge of racism as best I could. So after my blood pressure gradually returned to normal, I prepared myself to endure more walks through the streets of more small towns seeing the same looking sidewalks, the same looking roads. One thing was different, however. I had an enemy and I didn't know who it was.

DON'T VOTE FOR ME

CHAPTER X

WALKING THE WALK AND TALKING THE TALK

The Alma parade took me back on the road, meeting all my new friends again. Actually, I grew to like and admire my opponents. They seemed to treat me fairly. Maybe it was because I was not really a viable threat to them, but maybe it was because I treated them with respect. I was the only candidate to confess publicly at the debates that I thought each one of them would make a fine representative for our district, but of course I always added that I would make a better one. It turned out to be another splendid summer morning, but very hot that Alma parade day. *Hallelujah!* I had a group of supporters with me this time! But as the parade progressed they were way ahead of my pace. Again I did nothing but hand out brochures. I had no time for introductions, or small talk, and for the third straight parade I did not shake anyone's hand. At least it was a germ-free event. I felt like John Kerry, who is reputed to object to the customary political greeting of handshaking. I have no objection whatsoever; I just didn't have the opportunity to do it. After the parade the rest of my party returned home while I remained behind for several hours just to hang around and familiarize myself more with the city of Alma.

During the campaign, Mayor Paul Opsommer of Dewitt constantly crowed about his city having achieved the honor of

DON'T VOTE FOR ME

being named in the top 50 American communities in some magazine, or some such propaganda. Don't get me wrong, Dewitt is a fine town, but it was only fifth population-wise in the district, smaller than St. Johns, Alma, St. Louis, and Ithaca. Dewitt's advantage and disadvantage was its proximity to Lansing. It had seen explosive growth in residential development, but Alma had a lot going for itself as well, in spite of its refinery deconstruction. Alma has a beautiful river, a fine college, wonderful neighborhoods, some light industry, nice parks, and the expansive Michigan Masonic Home. I biked around town a bit that afternoon. It was sad to see some industrial blight along its riverfront, reminding people my age, of days gone by. I had a long conversation with an older man that had an extensive garden near the river's power relay station. We talked about things neither of us could do much about. Just where are we heading as Americans? What is our pilgrim journey? He believed in survival, self-sufficiency. His present and future was canning and jarring his vegetables. He was employed in planting and harvesting, storing and saving. He wanted to be seen as an example. He had a story to tell. And I could see that his story would outlast the unprepared. I really don't know why I found him interesting. Maybe it was because he didn't ask anything of me, or of government. So why should I have bothered to ask him to vote for me?

After that conversation, it being hot and I being prudent, I tarried back to the beer tent. Roger Kahn, the Republican senatorial candidate was tending bar. I, being the less serious

DON'T VOTE FOR ME

candidate, had two light beers to his one, and we discussed Michigan politics. I got the impression he was not an ideologue, but rather a leader, a facilitator, and one who might get things done between the parties. As I began to leave, a table full of revelers called to me and invited me to come over and talk with them. I informed them I was from St. Johns and that I remembered a few Alma names from high school sports back in the early 1970s. They knew a few of the athletes I had competed against back in the day. Anyhow, they said any candidate who had beer with them was their guy and I'd get their vote for sure. My money was on their beer -that was the sure thing. If only their beer could vote and not just talk... well, at least the beer was cold.

The following weekend the whole gaggle of candidates lined up again at Elsie. We all wound up our machines and rolled down another Main Street walking the same old walk. But soon I spied an unusual figure off to my left, not far from the start of the parade. There was a boy in an obvious vegetative state, staring blankly at us and we paraded before him. He was expressionless in his wheelchair, but he had the most angelic of faces and the bluest of eyes. I walked right up to him, not really sure if he was a puppet or a doll. What was he seeing, experiencing, and thinking? *Anything?* I handed a brochure to his caretaker, and I quickly moved on without an answer to questions kept to myself. My youngest son was doing back flips throughout the parade route. I was proud of him. He brought more attention to my campaign that day than anything I had done in any of the other parades. And then

DON'T VOTE FOR ME

halfway through the route I ran out of brochures. *Now I had no excuse!* I could shake hands! But then I did a John Kerry! I found that I had gone so long without pressing the flesh I couldn't bring myself to start! So I just walked and waved on yet another beautiful wasted Michigan summer day. In hindsight, I believe there was some value; the one enduring image of the Elsie parade was that of the wheelchair bound boy and his caretakers. I couldn't forget them.

More and more I was able to focus on the light at the end of the tunnel. It illuminated a world I once knew and underappreciated. There was real life there. I reflected on my sacrifices. That entire summer, for the first time in nearly twenty years, the Detroit Tigers were destroying the field in the American League, and I had seen but one game. To mollify my sense of missing out, at each parade I wore a Tigers cap with the olde English "D." I hadn't been up to the family cottage the entire summer. My family hadn't taken a real vacation. All the great summer weather was expended on campaigning.

Throughout the summer, I visited various groups. Early in the campaign I spoke with the Greenbush Township board and the citizens who gathered there. They graciously allowed me an opportunity to speak. That was my first public appearance. I was very nervous. I knew most of the people there and it was a little weird to get on the soapbox in front of them. I managed to recruit a fine worker who attended the meeting, and got a warm response from the board. Afterwards, I was invited to stay for the remainder

DON'T VOTE FOR ME

of the meeting, which involved their regular business agenda. I said, *"Sure, why not?"* Almost immediately, one citizen began to complain to them about a monetary pittance the board had approved to repair the hall's porch roof. Since it was a moot point, the chairman proceeded down the agenda but the disgruntled citizen wouldn't easily give in. He demanded to know why the GM jobs bank people couldn't fix it for free and save the township a few hundred bucks. The board replied they had already looked into it, but that particular program had come to an end. The citizen didn't want to accept that irrefutable answer, so the little debate didn't stop there. Right in the middle of it all, I got up and excused myself from the meeting saying, *"Well, I am not quite so sure I want to get elected after all... now I see what I am in for!"* The dissident citizen roared with laughter. He was one of those difficult, impish citizens who apparently delight in provoking elected officials simply for entertainment. They take up time, but they aren't likely to take up arms. They don't take politics too seriously, but they love to play the role of a pest.

I saw more than one like him. In Ithaca for example one guy demanded of me *"just what I was going to do about Daylight Savings Time?"* Hmmm. I guess I just don't know. Reset my watch?

When I visited the Fulton Township board, I had one of my more bizarre encounters. One of their board members insisted that I, as their state representative, *"give them the right to balance their budget!"*

88

DON'T VOTE FOR ME

Well that was a new one. What the heck did that mean? *"Okay,"* I said, playing along with the fiction that I was his state representative, instead of incumbent Scott Hummel. I majestically proclaimed, *"You sir! You have the right to balance your budget!"*

"Well, we can't," he insisted.

"Why not?" I replied. I was truly puzzled by this man's grievance.

"Because you stole our money from us! What are you going to do about it?" he demanded.

Well then I got it. He was talking about cuts in state revenue sharing for the local government units. *"Well,"* I told him, *"the state has a constitutional mandate to balance its budget, and if you want more revenue sharing, then there are only a few options the state has: either raise taxes, or increase revenues through an economic resurgence in the state's economy."*

As you can imagine, my answer didn't satisfy him. *"Stealing is just wrong,"* he said, and he *"couldn't support me as his representative unless I was willing to promise to give him their money back!"*

Okie-dokie. So much for sharing the pain and biting the bullet.

On another occasion, I spoke with a veterans group at the

DON'T VOTE FOR ME

VFW in Fowler. I was told afterwards that of all the candidates who had come their way that I was the only one who told it like it was. I appreciated hearing that.

I spoke with senior groups at Hazel Findlay in St. Johns and the senior center in Ithaca, both of which were delightful experiences -good for the soul- but not much help in the way of gathering votes. My appearances were more a diversion for them. They really only wanted the free plastic cups I brought, emblazoned with the *"Hayes for State Representative"* logo. They went like hot cakes. You would have thought a few of these seniors had been forced to cup their hands under the faucet to quench their thirst!

There were a couple of other issues I occasionally had to address with voters. Besides affirmative action and gay marriage, there was another so-called issue on the ballot that election year of 2006. It was the all important voter initiative to restore Michigan's ban on mourning dove hunting. I am not a hunter, and I suppose I like mourning doves as much as the next guy, but this was ridiculous. It soon became a politically-charged animal rights vs. hunting rights matter, rather than a debate on the merits. From my perspective, there should have been no debate. Hunting is legal and regulated, and once in a while I must admit it is right to delegate this sort of decision to the appropriate governmental agency, in this case the Michigan Department of Natural Resources. Anyhow, I informed the various groups that brought up the subject that I was going to exercise my right not to vote on

DON'T VOTE FOR ME

this particular issue, and let those who care more than me decide this crucial issue among themselves. Like a lot of things in politics, this matter was for the birds.

Finally, high on the list of voter concerns was the ongoing dumping of mountains of Canadian trash in our State's landfills. Lanes of semis carrying boxcars of Ontario's garbage and waste crossed our border daily to deposit their refuse here. Thirty years prior, in 1976, Michigan voters enacted the Nation's most stringent mandatory recycling program with our ten-cent bottle and can deposit law. That law was passed by us to curb waste, lessen the need for landfill space, and to promote energy and resource conservation. We were decades ahead of everyone in America in those regards until U.S. and Canadian business and governmental entities stuck their middle fingers in our face and forced us to involuntarily watch our land become a trash-heap as a result of a strange free trade interpretation of NAFTA. Once again, the federal government unwittingly stymied something good at the state level. An absurd way of governance trumped the will of the people. I promised to do all I could to bring an end to this practice of dumping. I had actually thought of blocking one of their trucks at the Blue Water Bridge like the dissident at Tiananmen Square, but I didn't. I guess I love Canadians more than I hate their trash. Looking back, perhaps I should have done it anyhow, and risk deportation or arrest. I didn't walk the talk.

Thankfully Michigan's U.S. Senators Carl Levin and Debbie Stabenow did wonders by negotiating an end to the

DON'T VOTE FOR ME

importation of Canadian residential waste in 2011, but commercial and industrial waste still cross our border daily, so it remains a problem. My point is that it should never have become a subject of international law, because it never should have happened in the first place. As a result Michiganders find ourselves decades behind, and now we have to clean up someone else's mess.

Even though I felt like I said all I had to say, there was more talking and more walking to do. Less than two weeks remained, and I thought I had seen and heard it all. I could not have been more mistaken.

DON'T VOTE FOR ME

CHAPTER XI
I CONFRONT MY ACCUSER

On Thursday, July 27 the last debate was held. For the first time, Democrats Rodney Hampton and Ron McComb were to appear on stage with the six Republican candidates at Alma College. Again, there was Gratiot County press coverage, but that was it. The moderator was objective and all of the questions were simple and fair, except for one I misunderstood which concerned a local brownfield energy park proposal and the technical multi-agency hurdles the government put in place to block or delay its development. To that question I gave my first truly made-up answer. My response was as confusing as a Sparky Anderson post-game press conference, and I said something amounting to "that proposal ain't not gone nowhere." I was totally clueless, but I managed to orally scribble a page or two of gibberish hoping to impress the professor and score points with volume if not content.

The debate highlights were humorous. Democrat Ron McComb made the extraordinary admission that he thought very seriously of not running for office at all because he had so much respect for Republican candidate Mike Trebesh. Then he added, *"If I hadn't entered the Democratic primary, I would be definitely supporting Republican Mike Trebesh."* But even more amazing was that Ron's young daughter, who accompanied him to the debate, began enthusiastically applauding …but she was not cheering on her dad. Instead, she was clapping for Mike Trebesh!

DON'T VOTE FOR ME

One question involved the expansion of CAFO's, agricultural feedlots and right to farm legislation. Everyone jumped to the defense of the farmers. *"Government is too intrusive. I support right to farm legislation. You need to be free to feed the people,"* blah, blah, blah. You know the script. I was the only candidate to suggest a policy that while society should be more than willing to forgive an accidental discharge of agricultural waste here and there, we cannot let our environment be continually abused by bad agricultural practices.

Paul Opsommer, as he was wont to do, bragged on and on about how he had just attended a major ag-expo in Fowler, making darn sure the audience was well aware that he was one of the only candidates invited to attend, and that some of the manure spreading machines were enormous, costing $250,000 or more- and best of all he was allowed to operate one of them that day! Paul is a very decent guy and I consider him a friend of mine, but political humility was not in his repertoire that summer. And Tim Black was about to kick a big boot load of well-deserved crap in Paul's direction.

"Paul," he said, *"you weren't the only one there. I was at that same ag-expo in Fowler. And everyone there agreed that no one could spread the manure better than you!"*

There was a pregnant pause, and then the whole auditorium erupted with belly laughs, but no one laughed harder than his Republican opponents. The expression that came over Paul's face

DON'T VOTE FOR ME

appeared like he had just taken a big old bite of a cow patty burger! *Oh my! Was Tim's quip funny!* It was truly a classic campaign moment. We all shared a simmering, lingering jealousy about Paul's Michigan RTL PAC endorsement. We had all suffered under the weight of Paul's advantages that summer, but in spite of his ego, money, signs, and endorsements he couldn't duck under that soft and fresh cow-pie that Tim Black smushed right between his eyes.

But there was more to come. We were asked about the breakdown in bipartisanship and what we would do to restore cooperation between the parties. All professed an earnest desire to promote unity and good citizenship, but within minutes in response to another issue, Paul Opsommer gratuitously added a plug for Dick DeVos, the Republican gubernatorial candidate into his answer. Democrat Rodney Hampton countered Paul's endorsement of DeVos with one of his own for Democrats Jim Marcinkowski, Debbie Stabenow and Jennifer Granholm. When it was my turn, I glanced right and looked straight at Rodney and said, *"So much for all that talk of bipartisanship, eh Rodney?"*

Then turning slowly left toward Paul Opsommer, I paused and continued, *"Eh, Paul?"* Again the audience roared with their amused approval at the jab, loving it! It was proving to be a fun evening. I was enjoying the night immensely, especially as the underdog. The audience's appreciation of the humor made up for the many futile attempts to interest the public at large in our campaigns. The long ordeal would soon be over and this particular

DON'T VOTE FOR ME

night was providing some classic and memorable moments. And then at the end we were given a couple minutes each for our closing statements- our final thoughts in the final campaign debate forum. I was to follow the remarks of Rodney Hampton, and Rodney served me up a slow hanging breaking ball over the center of home plate and I crushed it out of the ballpark.

Here is how it happened: Republicans always love to quote Lincoln, or more recently Reagan, but Democrats worship the words of legendary John F. Kennedy. They do so with good reason -so many of his speeches were remarkable. Anyhow, Rodney gave a sincere, heartfelt, well-prepared closing, liberally laced with quotes attributed to JFK, with his impassioned call for service, duty and citizenship. The audience fell respectfully and contemplatively silent. Rodney ended with one final plea to heed JFK's legacy and to renew and rekindle the great American dream. It nearly caused me to reflect on the bridge we built back in 1963 on Sanborn Street.

Then it was my turn.

I purposefully paused when the moderator called my name. I grabbed the podium with both of my hands and with a tone of fatherly admonishment, turned very slowly and deliberately in Rodney's direction.

"Rodney," I said. *"I knew Jack Kennedy. I worked with Jack Kennedy. Jack Kennedy was a friend of mine. Rodney, you*

DON'T VOTE FOR ME

are no…"

I didn't need to go further. For the final time that evening the assembly rocked! *I had brought down the house with Lloyd Bentsen's zinger!* What an ending, even though it came at Rodney's expense. But I kind of liked Rodney. I respected his sincerity and campaign acumen.

He looked at me with a wry grin and eyes that said, *"You got me. I deserved it."*

I wanted him to know there was absolutely nothing personal about my quip, so I went over to his chair, shook his hand and slapped him on the back.

Ten minutes later I wanted to deck him.

After the debate, I was in the highest spirits, higher than I had ever been in my reluctant campaign for office. Everyone seemed to be in a good mood, but Rodney seemed a bit sullen, standing next to his campaign manager. I thought he was taking the whole thing way too seriously. So I approached him once more and told him, *"I am sorry Rodney, but you gave me a slow 2-and-0 fastball over the middle of the plate with nothing on it."*

He glared at me and said, *"That's okay, 'Mr. Black Girls Shouldn't Be Having Babies'!"*

WHOA!!!!

DON'T VOTE FOR ME

The Earth itself instantly changed its polarity! The Rosetta stone had just spoken! The mystery was over! He was the source of the slander I suffered at the courthouse! My adrenaline skyrocketed and the Irish in me was ready to battle to the death.

"That was you?!" My voice was rising, along with my blood pressure.

"Yes, that was me. Are you denying you said that?"

"Hell yes, I deny that! I know I didn't say that! And you know it too!"

"Well, that's what my notes say," Rodney coolly responded.

"Big frickin' deal what your notes say! Your notes can say whatever you want them to say! This is bullshit, Rodney. Why didn't you call me for clarification first? Why didn't you check out my website and find out the truth about my positions? You would know I'm not saying anything different than what Jesse Jackson has been saying, but I'm saying it without regard to race!"

My website clearly reflected my belief that couples should have all the children they want. In fact, I think our national birth rate is far too low. I was not promoting a freeze on *"young, urban girls having babies"* or eugenics or anything remotely like it. I just wanted all of our youth to stop burdening themselves, their

DON'T VOTE FOR ME

children and our society with such a serious national problem until they found themselves in a position of accountability. I saw the results of this national tragedy every day played out in my job as assistant prosecutor.

Rodney insisted his version was accurate and called over his campaign assistant to support his claim, but those notes did not reflect any reference of mine to race. His notes corroborated my recollection, but I was still fighting mad.

"Rodney," I said, *"in two weeks I am going to lose this election, and after that I'll go back and work in the same place I have been working for 17 years. I have developed a reputation over that time. You tried to destroy all of that with one misquote on a matter taken out of context. I have absolutely no respect for you at all. In fact I think you are a coward. You are a creep. If this is what you think you need to do to win, to ruin another person's career to succeed, go ahead. Is that what all your talk of JFK is all about? You are a hypocrite."*

Somehow, my wife got into the middle of it, trying to play peacemaker. But I couldn't and wouldn't be appeased. Yet after the report from his campaign assistant, Rodney seemed to admit some doubt as to his recollection. That, together with my persistence, insistence, fortitude, and yes, aggression, persuaded him to reassess things. He promised to visit my website and to read my position statement. He said if he was wrong that he was sorry.

DON'T VOTE FOR ME

I said that wasn't good enough. He would have to undo the damage he had caused me by issuing a retraction to everyone, starting with the judge from whom I learned of the allegation. He agreed to those terms as well. Trust me, I didn't for a moment believe anything would ever happen, but I told him that if he did what he promised, he would regain all of my respect. However I flat out told him I didn't think he had it in him.

The episode lasted about 10 minutes. It was without question the most animated encounter of my campaign. Amazingly very few of the people at Alma College had taken note of the incident, and the few who did, seemed unconcerned about it. They were all in their own spheres of influence and innocuous to it. As I was leaving, I ran into the Gratiot County Republican Chairman. He saw some of my tirade toward Rodney and he inquired about it. I told him my side of the situation. He commented that he had gotten word the Democrats were going to play real dirty in this election.

I replied to him, *"All that matters to me is that Rodney keeps his word."* If he did, I told him, I too would keep my end of the bargain and Rodney would garner my greatest respect, but we both agreed that was highly unlikely. In fact, I didn't give it the slightest chance.

At the end of the day I had had enough. I lost all faith. I could no longer bring myself to believe in the American political system. It was long past time to quit caring about those things I

DON'T VOTE FOR ME

believed in as a child. JFK, RFK, MLK …all of it was indeed just a fairy tale after all. You don't get to live happily ever after. In reality you get assassinated. The cynics were right. I just didn't care anymore, and even with all the drama after the debate, I slept very well that night. I made my peace. I was content to be buried in my political grave with the truth. Politics -one of my great loves in life- was dead to me, and I was indifferent to the loss.

****

But overnight somehow, someway time turned back. To Sanborn Street. St. Mary's. Garfield Elementary. To a bunch of working-class Protestant and Catholic boys and girls, together building a bridge over a small crick to honor a man and a nation who inspired them to work instead of play on their day off of school.

Yes. It did. When the sun rose, I woke up to my roller coaster ride dumping me into the ice-cold blue waters of the Lake Huron of my youth. Just as Sister Timothy promised, miracles can happen. I thought I must have been still dreaming when I awoke to find that Rodney emailed me a copy of a statement, plus his email list. In his letter he directed his Democratic supporters to my website for all to read my complete position regarding the issue of teenage out-of-wedlock births.

The letter read:

DON'T VOTE FOR ME

Democrats,

I am issuing a formal retraction of the quotes that I attributed to Republican candidate Kevin Hayes. I distributed these quotes in an email that I sent last week, and may have also mentioned them at the Gratiot County Democratic Party meeting this Tuesday. Although both I and one of my campaign volunteers took notes at the Republican debate in Ithaca, and believe we correctly transcribed what was said, I have been informed by Mr. Hayes that I am in error. In fairness to Mr. Hayes, I and my campaign intern were sitting in the back of the room. Mr. Hayes said that he was cut off by the moderator and disagrees that he said these things as I have written them. I have offered to turn over both my notes as well as my volunteer's notes to Mr. Hayes for review and this offer will remain open.

Mr. Hayes would like you to know that his full position on any issue can be found at his website, but in particularly [sic] he said to refer you specifically to "Babies Having Babies."

If you have any questions about Mr. Hayes' positions, you can contact him through his website, email or phone.

In reflection, I should have spoke with Kevin before publishing these quotations. In the future I will contact other candidates before publishing a direct quotation.

I APOLOGIZE PUBLICLY FOR ANY DIFFICULTY

DON'T VOTE FOR ME

THAT THIS HAS CAUSED HIM IN HIS PERSONAL OR PROFESSIONAL LIFE.

[Emphasis in the original]

I am not sending this email to you BCC because I want Mr. Hayes to see that I have given this the same wide distribution as the original message. I apologize to you for exposing your email address like this and will return to sending you emails BCC after this incident has passed.

Thank you,

Rodney Hampton

I was happily... well, stunned! His letter wasn't a complete confession of guilt, but it was far better than anything I could have hoped for. After all, I must admit the incomplete remark I made in Ithaca could have been easily and conveniently misinterpreted. By doing what he did, Rodney had redeemed himself with me, and then some.

I immediately emailed Rodney a thank you. He kindly replied, admitting that this whole episode was probably the greatest error in his campaign. Anyhow, as far as I was concerned, the fire was out and the smoke had completely cleared. My reputation was now restored to the status quo ante, and I was ready to return to my day job for good. I felt like an Earthling again.

DON'T VOTE FOR ME

Yes, Rodney was wrong about me, and I was right to passionately defend myself. But let me confess: I was wrong about Rodney too. I have a penchant for putting my foot in my mouth occasionally and I jump to conclusions too. We all do. All of us are wrong at times. That is why the good Creator of the universe gave us a way to move towards a more perfect union through contrition and forgiveness. After all, we are created equal …not perfect.

DON'T VOTE FOR ME

CHAPTER XII
HAIL MARYS AND SUPER BOWLS

There was little left to do. Another parade in Fowler, a few more literature drops and then it would be over. The Fowler parade was a celebration engineered by the village's *Most Holy Trinity Church*. I ran into Tim Black. I informed him that just days before I received a campaign letter from his great aunt, a letter that happened to be addressed from a nun's retirement home in northern Wisconsin. In it the nun lauded Tim's goodness, kind heart and his general Catholic godliness. I said to Tim, *"I didn't know you were Catholic."*

He said, *"Well, I am sort of."*

I replied, *"Well, I have never seen you in church. What parish do you go to?"*

"Well, I don't," he said with a fair amount of satisfaction. *"But that was a great letter from my aunt, wasn't it?"*

"Tim, don't you think that is pretty misleading?" Maybe it was irreligious, but I couldn't help but chuckle. Ever the honorable 29 year old statesman, Tim just laughed along with me.

As Paul Opsommer passed the throng waiting in front of the town's splendid Catholic church, over the loudspeaker it was

105

DON'T VOTE FOR ME

announced of course that Paul had the RTL endorsement. They might as well have said he won the primary. They didn't mention anything about farm expos or manure spreading in Fowler, just for the record.

The following weekend was the last of the campaign. *St. Cyril's* and the village of Bannister had a big Czech-Slovak celebration, with the ZBCJ hall serving an excellent meal. I passed out hundreds of my last pieces of campaign literature –an 8 ½" x 11" single sheet of yellow paper. Most of the people were not residents of the district, but I brought enough for everyone. It read:

Dear Citizen:

Throughout the course of my campaign for the 93rd District I've asked only one thing regarding your choice for State Representative:

Don't vote for me unless you are willing to shoulder your share of the load.

No other candidate has said that. I have because we are living in precarious times and we need to wake up. One OPEC embargo and we will see the wailing and gnashing of teeth throughout our land. If that happens we will have no one to blame but ourselves. For decades now we have not heeded the warning call to become energy self-sufficient. We are at least ten years behind where we need to be, and we can't afford to waste

DON'T VOTE FOR ME

another day.

We are too willing to defend nations who disrespect us, to turn a blind eye toward illegal immigration, and to support multinational corporations who are disloyal to us. This must stop. I have decided to get off the sidelines and do something about it. One of my goals as your State Representative will be the development of energy production in our district and throughout the nation. For thirty years we've survived a policy of neglect. Our energy dependence cannot be cured overnight, but once we commit ourselves to domestic production good jobs will be created and we will be a better nation for it.

No other candidate will demand more from you. We must work together. Now I ask again:

Are you willing to do your part?

If so, vote for me August 8th. Vote for me if you want to be part of the solution. We need to return to our principles. We need to put America and Americans first.

That message encapsulated my entire campaign and I am content to include it here for posterity.

I ran into Tim Black at this final event as well. Maybe he *was* rejoining the church. Anyhow, I informed him that just the day before I had received a strange *"robo"* phone call at home.

DON'T VOTE FOR ME

The recorded message claimed Tim Black was a closet Democrat or a communist or some such nonsense. I hung up on the ridiculous message before it finished. Anyhow, Tim just laughed it off. Then curiously he added, *"Didn't you hear about the other calls?"*

I had no idea what he was talking about.

"Yeah," he continued, *"there are calls like that going out about everyone but you and Carlson."*

I said, *"That's weird, because I didn't get any calls except for the one about you."*

I was confused. Why were people getting recorded calls about the other candidates, but not the two of us? And why didn't I get a call about Opsommer, Trebesh or Nunez? But it didn't seem like a big deal, just bizarre.

Unbeknownst to me there was already a firestorm of reaction brewing from the other three candidates. Someone had clearly orchestrated a devious last minute plan to sway the campaign. It wasn't long before most, if not all of their fingers pointed in the direction of the Black campaign. It was highly coincidental to them that these robo calls seemed to be designed solely to increase Black's advantage among unidentified voters. The disinformation in the calls concerning Tim Black seemed relatively benign compared to the slanderous things being said

DON'T VOTE FOR ME

about Mike Trebesh, Paul Opsommer and Josh Nunez. Further, it was claimed that the anti-Black recordings seemed to be dialed only to primary voters who were already identified as voting for someone other than Black himself.

These robo calls garnered the immediate attention of the press, but whoever orchestrated the attacks covered their tracks well. A reporter who covered the story from Gratiot County called me about the situation. I told her I had shrugged off the messages as infantile and ridiculous disinformation that no-right thinking person could possibly believe. I only lamented that apparently Greg Carlson and I were not important enough to be included in the wave of recorded attacks. I needed the publicity. One thing was indisputable: as the other three candidates justly complained, Tim Black was found defending himself. I called Nunez, Opsommer and Trebesh to tell each of them that I would do anything they asked of me to set their record straight. Otherwise, I stayed out of the fray and made no accusations. Nevertheless the calls were totally unwarranted. They were mean-spirited, and contrary to what had been until then a very clean campaign among the Republicans candidates in the primary.

The recorded messages thereafter seemed to die out quickly, only to resurrect on Election Day. A final blitzkrieg of robo calls purportedly coming from the Opsommer campaign reminded voters to get out and vote for him. These calls were repetitively made over and over and over all through the night before the election, and continued throughout Election Day as

DON'T VOTE FOR ME

well.

Opsommer called me at the Prosecutor's Office about the matter, and I advised my boss of the situation. The word spread quickly that yet again another candidate was being victimized by these anonymous robo calls. It was truly a juvenile and demented conclusion to the primary election. Once again Tim Black stridently professed his innocence by email to all of the candidates, but I'm not sure when or if they were ever convinced by it. Regardless, no one was able to prove anything, and nothing could have been done about it at the time anyhow. The election was upon us all and the chips would fall where they may. It was never established who was behind the nefarious phone calls, but the scheme proved too little, too late. Throughout the district the word got out quickly to ignore the robo calls and in large measure they were.

Even so, Paul Opsommer felt a need, and had the funding, to contact every identifiable Republican voter with a robo call of his own. He left voters a telephonic message alerting them to the fact that his campaign was not responsible for the repetitive phone calls, and to remind them one more time that he was the only Republican who had the RTL endorsement -as if they didn't already know. Even I got his call on Election Day! Now, *that's* paranoia!

Well, like me, I think the voters had finally had enough. The last card had been dealt, the last bluff was called. I thanked

DON'T VOTE FOR ME

God above when Election Day, August 8, 2006, finally arrived. My only hope was that I would garner more than the 53 votes that had been set as the low water mark, as prophesized by my sister-in-law. Admittedly, I also hoped that I might not end up in last place, although I knew that was the likely outcome.

I went to work that day as always. I had no victory celebration planned. No party. No gathering at the house. No concession speech. Nothing. My wife and I went to a late movie in Lansing –a truly awful film starring Robin Williams called *The Night Listener*. When we got home, I checked the computer for the results. I saw I had lost badly. Though results still trickled in, Opsommer had won handily. I called Paul and left a message of congratulations and then I went to bed. While my wife fell asleep, I laid awake for several hours, haunted by my woeful effort. I confessed to myself and God that I had lost before I took one step. I knew that in my heart I let people down who took time to help me. I could not blame the voters. I had not done the things necessary to generate enthusiasm in advance of my candidacy. Maybe I was too extreme a centrist [*sic*], and primary voters like the edges of the spectrum. Whatever it was, I knew I had let down my family, former teachers, and yes, the voters of an area in this great country that is full of really good and decent people. No one likes to lose but I had it coming. I will never be able to say I gave it my best effort, but looking back, I can say just as honestly that it wouldn't have made any difference if I had. I would have lost no matter what. That was the political reality.

DON'T VOTE FOR ME

My mind wandered. What were these past twelve weeks all about? What did I learn from it? Was it an experience best forgotten, or was there something more to it? Should I write about my journey, to let people know what it was like, or would I be too chicken to even try? I had so few answers. For some reason I thought of that blue-eyed boy from the Elsie parade. He was the most innocent person I had ever seen. I thought of him as a person imprisoned through no choice of his own. What would he do if he only could? One thing was sure –you can bet he would do it all.

I finally dozed off to sleep. The next morning I called into work. I needed a mental health day. I told my secretary I needed a day off because my butt hurt from the spanking the voters gave me. She understood. It is true that everyone loves a winner, but everyone can relate to a 'loser', too. With a couple hundred signs to pick up, starting with the large 4x4 signs, I used the time to heal and self-medicate my emotional, clinically depressed state of being. Picking up the signs provided good and righteous therapy.

While out and about I saw Mike Trebesh performing the same ritual. I pulled into a drive off Dewitt Road and we shook hands and embraced. In the end all of his early efforts to gain an advantage went for naught. Losing had to be very tough on him, but he was calm and resigned to a new paradigm (which down-shifted once again in 2010 after he ran a unilaterally negative campaign for state senate and lost a primary election against current Lieutenant Governor Brian Calley). We parted ways and as the day came to its end, I had erased my name from the political

DON'T VOTE FOR ME

landscape of Michigan's 93rd State House District forever.

As it turned out, I got the 53 votes and even better, *I did not come in last place.* Otherwise things turned out about the way I thought they would. My dalliance with the world of politics was over, but I lost more than an election. Though I would have loved being in the legislature so I could bring a practicing lawyer's perspective, I lost my desire to get involved in politics again anytime soon.

I stayed out of things the rest of the way in 2006. I wasn't sure about Republicans or Democrats. I'm still not sure. Certainly there are a lot of good people in both parties, but somehow too many politicians have forgotten that the art of politics is not about getting what you *want*. It is about getting what you *can*.

That being said, I hope enough people in both parties may begin to practice a higher art. I beg you to become profiles in courage for our times, so that government of the people, by the people, and for the people, shall not perish from the earth. Unless those at the helm agree together to alter course, our economic ship of state appears to be headed in the direction of an unfortunate and mathematically certain outcome. Democrats *and* Republicans must find new and acceptable ways for government to serve the people, and do so within our means. I know I'm a little off track here, but I doubt these are just flitting thoughts from the heartland. I would venture to guess I am echoing thoughts from all over the country. I would be lying if I suggested otherwise.

DON'T VOTE FOR ME

Although so much blame is heaped upon our elected officials, I worry just as much, if not more, about us -the people of the United States of America. Can we do the math? Are we really willing and able to govern ourselves? Instead of merely complaining, will we also accept our role in problem solving? Are we worthy of our republican form of government? Of a representative democracy? Ultimately we get what we deserve. There is no guarantee, and once we lose it we are not likely to get it back. It will not be any easier than it was 235 years ago, that's for sure.

I have some last words of warning. Listen please. If our country strays from our traditional two party system, I hope we are wise enough as a people to demand runoff elections until the popular vote results in majority-rule elections. 50% plus one means something. It means a lot. There are too many pluralities in this country. The center must hold.

In spite of all my doubts I have one lasting hope. My former nemesis –a man I hated as much as anyone I've ever hated for ten minutes of my life - Rodney Hampton, was upset in his primary, losing in very tight race to Ron McComb. Rodney called me the day after the election. As I sat on the curb outside the Applebee's in East Lansing, I spent some time talking with him about things, commiserating I suppose. I felt sorry for him. He gave it his all, and he had come so close to winning. I hate to think that an incomplete thought of mine in an innocuous debate in the middle of nowhere may have served to bring an end to his political

DON'T VOTE FOR ME

aspirations, but I hope not. What he did the day after the Alma debate was extraordinary for our times. Maybe we both discovered something better for our souls than political victory. At least I know I did. The day after the general election, I wrote a letter and forwarded it to Rodney to share with his Democratic supporters. It read:

Dear Democratic Supporter:

I write to tell you of a remarkable episode between a Republican and a Democrat, an episode which I hope may repeat itself in various ways in future rivalries and campaigns so that it may not be called remarkable at all, but a matter of course which is common and expected from our politicians.

Rodney Hampton and I were candidates for the Michigan 93rd District for State House of Representatives as a Democrat and Republican respectively. While neither of us advanced beyond the primary election, we both know the experience of getting off the sidelines and entering the fray of battle. Each of us did this knowing it can get ugly in the mud and dirt in the field of politics.

But a good thing happened between us and I want you to know about it, even if it is from my perspective. It may be difficult, if not impossible, for voters to understand what candidates endure. Much is expected. Much is demanded. And in today's sound-bite system much is misheard and

DON'T VOTE FOR ME

misrepresented.

I confronted Rodney about such a circumstance in the course of our campaign. To Rodney's great credit he took the time and effort to rectify the damage that I had suffered not as a candidate, but as a human being.

He has earned my respect. And when he called me the day following our mutual defeats in our respective primary elections, I was able to listen, and listen well. We are not always that far apart that we should not hear of how much we are the same.

May God Bless,

Kevin Hayes

I don't know if my letter softened any hearts, but I hope so. Too often people like to think the worst of others. We are pretty quick to judge these days it seems. We don't have to be that way. It is neither good for us nor good for our country.

A week or so after the general election, the winner Paul Opsommer invited me to one final victory celebration. I accepted. That was nice of him. He deserved to win. He has gone on to become an exemplary member of the state legislature. He has been re-elected twice, and because of term limits he is now in his final term as state representative. That is a shame.

DON'T VOTE FOR ME

With the 2010 census complete, the 93rd State House district will live on as an entirely reconfigured political subdivision due to reapportionment. I don't know have any idea who will become the next state representative, but it won't be me. Quite often the best part of losing some intangible thing is coming to the humbling conclusion that perhaps it was never meant to be. It doesn't hurt to acknowledge the possibility that the hand of the good God might have been at work. Maybe you are just being pushed in another direction. Maybe you are being shoved out of the way of a landmine.

With a heavy heart I've struggled whether or not to include -or even try to write- these next few lines, so please forgive this parting thunderbolt from out of the blue. I was not the one from my campaign who needed Providence's helping hand after all. I was never in any real danger, and I didn't need a push in another direction. If nothing else, I knew I could find my way back home. But now I know the full extent of the blessings afforded by the latter kind of intervention. I know the converse as well. Though I am not yet able to adequately express the waves of emotive epiphanies which haunted and inspired me last fall in Ward 57 at Walter Reed in our nation's capital, I live in the hope that before I die I may see my oldest son run the bases just once more with joy, like he did when he was a kid, like Bill Mazeroski. I would like to have Bill sitting next to me watching it. But it is OK with me if it never happens. Thank God it was a phone call from Afghanistan, not a knock at the door. Yet, maybe there was some divine

DON'T VOTE FOR ME

guidance, for it could have been worse. It always can. I am a witness to it. I have friends who got that knock instead. I won't ask for more.

For now, suffice it to say that I am infinitely more grateful for my family and for those who defend my country than ever before, not to mention everything else I have always taken for granted. And you know what else? When I think of all the places on this planet where I might have been born I realize how lucky I am. It is no wonder so many people from all over the world want to come here and live. Yeah, you bet I want to keep it that way. People *should* aspire to become Americans. By the very nature of our creation, we are a people conceived in liberty and born to dream. As Bobby Kennedy once suggested, why not? We ought to become better citizens. We ought to dream again, with open eyes.

Let me conclude by being *more* perfectly clear than I was in the beginning. I was wrong. You and I may feel like nobodies, but together we aren't. We The People have been endowed with the most amazing gifts. You can even run for office. Don't be afraid. Just don't follow my example.

On the other hand, maybe things didn't turn out to be so bad after all. Those purgative twelve weeks all too often seemed like an eternity. But in truth, looking back, it was just a sliver of time. Maybe I am a better man for it. From the beginning, I knew my chances were as bleak as George Plimpton tossing a winning

DON'T VOTE FOR ME

touchdown pass in a Super Bowl. Besides, it doesn't always matter whether you come out the winner. What matters is that you have a story to tell.

So, here is mine. I am now 57 years old, and it has finally dawned on me why the child I once was had so much faith growing up in these United States. We celebrate the good in both the common and uncommon man. Our Founders bequeathed a means of self-determination to everyone, with liberty as our cornerstone. Though the years have quickly passed the beauty of freedom never fades.

My political adventure may not have seemed like a pursuit of happiness, but now I smile and laugh about it. Maybe some of you haven't found happiness yet, but no one can stop you from trying. It's up to you. As our little journey together comes to its end I leave this bridge of words for you, and to our nation's posterity. I'm going to cross it and I'm not looking back. The future calls. I have come to understand what it means to be an American, again.

And that, Ladies and Gentlemen, is what I learned.

The End

DON'T VOTE FOR ME

APPENDIX

2006 PRIMARY ELECTION RESULTS:

REPUBLICANS:

PAUL OPSOMMER 2,664

MIKE TREBESH 1,653

TIM BLACK 1,498

JOSH NUNEZ 1,431

KEVIN HAYES 652

GREG CARLSON 492

DEMOCRATS:

RON McCOMB 1,517

RODNEY HAMPTON 1,368

2006 GENERAL ELECTION RESULTS:

PAUL OPSOMMER 20,700

RON McCOMB 16,049

DON'T VOTE FOR ME

EPILOGUE

I dedicated this story to my son, Specialist Matthew Hayes, who serves his country in the United States Army. On September 17, 2010, near Kunduz, Afghanistan, Spc. Hayes stepped on an IED anti-personnel mine while assisting a Navy EOD team when detection devices failed. As a result he lost his right leg below his knee, among other injuries.

He is continuing rehabilitation and physical therapy with the 10th Mountain Division in upstate New York, after his recent discharge from the Walter Reed Army Medical Center in Washington, D.C. The iconic Army hospital compound closed in the summer of 2011, but for those who encountered the somber radiance of its timeless shadows over the past 102 years, its gates shut only to the visible world.

He was one of the last U.S. servicemen to be treated at old Walter Reed. His injuries resulted from Taliban activities to suppress voter participation during Afghanistan's national elections. Mines were being cleared that day by U.S. servicemen so that Afghan citizens could go to the polls and vote.

Contact information:

Kevin Hayes

Hayes & Hyde Press

1210 W. Hyde Rd.

St. Johns, MI 48879

USA

Tele: 517.490.8695

Email: kevinbrennanhayes@gmail.com

Web: www.hayesandhyde.com

By the Same Author

Kickland (fiction)

Christi's Not Afraid (unpublished children's story)

Amrit's Sin of 2pi (unpublished short story)

ABOUT THE AUTHOR

Born and raised in Michigan, Kevin Hayes attended grade school in Port Huron and middle school in Flint, before graduating from St. Johns High School. He is an alumnus of Michigan State University with a B.A. in political science. While working at the Michigan Republican State Committee, he co-chaired the Reagan-Bush Commitment '80 campaign in Michigan. He earned his J.D. from the Thomas M. Cooley Law School, where he clerked for the Honorable Thomas E. Brennan, former Chief Justice of the Michigan Supreme Court and founder of Cooley Law School. He is a lawyer with 25 years of service as an assistant prosecutor in Clare, Barry, and Clinton County.

He was first published at the age of 14 in Parade magazine, earning five dollars for his question to author George Plimpton. In addition to his interest in UFO's, politics and the Detroit Tigers, he had the karmic experience of travelling extensively throughout northern India as part of Rotary International's group study exchange in 1989. He has completed more than a dozen cross-country ski marathons, most notably the North American Vasa, held annually in Traverse City, Michigan, and the American Birkebeiner, held in Hayward, Wisconsin. He is a member and union steward with Public Employees Representative Association, Local 100. He is married and the father of four children. He has two grandchildren.